Thatcher Thayer

Lectures and Sermons, 1882

Thatcher Thayer

Lectures and Sermons, 1882

ISBN/EAN: 9783337114541

Printed in Europe, USA, Canada, Australia, Japan

Cover: Foto ©Lupo / pixelio.de

More available books at **www.hansebooks.com**

AND

SERMONS

BY

T. THAYER.

1882.

NEWPORT
T. T. PITMAN, PRINTER
1887.

PRIVATELY PRINTED.

THE VICARIOUS ELEMENT IN NATURE AND ITS RELATION TO CHRIST.

PRELIMINARY VIEWS.

ANYTHING done or suffered by one instead of another, or simply representing another, is vicarious. The word describes what is plainly within our observation. It admits various degrees and different forms. It may signify substitution in the most exhaustive sense, as where one literally, whether by choice or compulsion, consciously or unconsciously, takes the place of another, for good or evil. As this is the fullest, so is it the simplest meaning. The same idea is expressed with less fullness by representativeness, as when one represents another and decides for him. This term is more indefinite, ranging almost from identification with another to determining for him in general. Representativeness, too, may be free or constrained, conscious or unconscious. A still more indefinite and general sense of the vicarious is illustrated when one acts on another's account, yet not in any manner of substitution or representativeness. The idea of the vicarious is not indeed abruptly limited, but gradually disappears. Practically there is no difficulty in recognizing it even in its faintest expression.

Now it is admitted that a vicarious element pervades the revelation of Jesus Christ. Even those who hold to the least possible of the supernatural in him, and some who have only vague faith in him as the most eminent of men, still apply the word vicarious to him, while they object to any full sense of it. Those who believe in the supernatural being of the Lord Jesus Christ, give more distinct prominence to his work as vicarious. And yet even here is great diversity as to the degree of fullness of that vicarious element. Some understand Christ to be revealed as literally in the place of sinful man, completely fulfilling the idea of substitution. This is largely the language of the great confessions. This describes the view of a very considerable class of theologians now, who do not see sufficient reasons for abandoning this utmost significance of Christ's vicarious work. It is also the view of a multitude of believers, who, without questioning its theological aspects, simply receive this full meaning as most expressive of what Christ is to them. For indeed it may be claimed for the unqualified sense of Christ's sufferings as vicarious, that it most identifies him with the soul, conscious of its wants. It is the complete conception of the incarnation. It brings Christ into wondrous nearness to us, and aside from the question of its scriptural authority will always have peculiar attraction for some minds. But many shrink from this, and do not believe it taught in scripture. These, however, recognize more or less representativeness in Christ. With various modifications they believe in his propitiatory sacrifice and in justification through faith in him. Others interpret the scripture doctrine of redemption in a more general way still. In all these views the vicarious idea is preserved as characterizing the incarnation. It may fairly be asserted that the mass of christendom has so understood scripture. Indeed in every age christians have cherished, with the most particular reverence and delight, the vicarious aspect of Christ. Against this, objections have been offered, and to meet these, the form of doctrine has been variously presented. These objections have, in a measure, assumed that what was vicarious was arbitrary and peculiar to Christ. We leave now what pertains to Christ's work and kingdom as matters of pure revelation, "heavenly things," as he termed them, and consider what he discriminated as "earthly things," such as man's actual moral character and state and relations and wants and modes of being and development These are independent of revelation, and within the scope of our observation revelation indeed throws authoritative light on man, still we study him in the sphere of nature and contrasted with the supernatural. Now if the vicarious instead of being originally and arbitrarily employed in the work of Christ, be found a condition of human being and so uniformly present in human development as to be necessary to our conception of man, this will very seriously affect our consideration of certain objections to the doctrine of Christ as generally held. Besides it will open some important aspects of christian morality. The subject of investigation then, be it kept in mind, is human nature, as it is proved beyond question to be in its fundamental relations and social proceedings. Notice particularly, this is considering man in society. There is indeed no other man for us. The vicarious element cannot exist except in related existence. Again our enquiries do not regard man merely as degenerate, but in any state. True, the effect of a change from one moral state to another must be very great. Moral evil, whenever and however it came to be in human nature, must have produced results impossible to estimate. It cannot, however, have altered the essential constitution of man. This must be independent of both moral good and moral evil for either to be in it. Whatever the moral quality of the person, whether it remains as at first, or is radically changed, this constitution and its modes must remain the same. If this be not so it were hard to fix upon the identical in human nature. There is no risk in saying that it is impossible for us to conceive of human nature other than what it is, whether morally good or morally evil. Into this view will enter those surroundings which though not essential to humanity, are commonly connected with it. Now it is believed that the more this human nature is studied, the more it will show of the vicarious in its inmost structure and in its developments. This is the more striking because, as we shall see, it often acts thus unconsciously. In pursuing these investigations there is no danger of lessening the distinction between the natural and the supernatural, nor of taking anything from the originality of Christ's redemption. The tendency to get rid of difficulties by confounding distinctions is indeed very noticeable in certain directions of modern thought, and the worst instance of this is lowering the dignity of Christ's person and lessening the greatness of his salvation by bringing him nearer the level of earthly benefactors. We cannot exalt him too highly nor regard his work too exclusively, for it is above all works of men, in the highest sense original and apart. But there is possible such a treatment of the relations of truths in nature to those of pure revelation, as to honor and confirm the supernatural.

It does not injure the conception of the supernatural to find it harmonizing with the natural. Human redemption by Christ, is not qualified in the least by a mode already existing in human nature, which should be employed in that redemption, and might seem almost to have prefigured the manner of Christ's manifestation, as the earthern mould prefigures the form that shall fill it. On the contrary, to find in the divine interposition such use of the structure of human nature now incapable of its own restoration, as to employ its own modes to restore it, such fulfillment and crowning of them as natural types, is rather a great confirmation of the glorious Being in whom these attain their complete significance. Nor must it remain unnoticed that in this correspondence of human nature to Christ's mode of redemption, there is manifest a unity which renders objections to that mode equally valid against what exists in humanity itself. Should our study of the constitution of human nature and its modes of action, result in the conclusion that it is pervaded by a vicarious element, our actual world will have increased significance. For it will by its very processes, suggest and illustrate and confirm what revelation shall declare as a divine method. It is not presumption to expect that the humanity into which a redeemer should enter, would be found to have a structure and development answering to his mode of redemption, and the world in which he was to accomplish his great work should have analogies and correspondencies in harmony with it, unconscious types in nature itself. And perhaps some day it may form matter of adoring recognition, that as a revealed ritual was given to lead men to Christ by preparing them to accept a vicarious Saviour, human nature itself in its actual workings, on a larger scale forms a vast pedagogy to the same end.

The Vicarious in the Structure of Society and Representativeness in Race.

THE expression "structures of society" is offensive to some because it is used by certain writers in a way that appears to ignore any free will in the individual. This plainly tends to materialize everything human—of course all moral quality must be finally given up. This is one extreme. We do well to recoil from what leads to such conclusions. But there may be an excessive reaction from this. So it is that some, repelled by an exaggerated statement of structure in society, are almost ready to deny any at all. Hence comes a vague way of looking at society as if it proceeded very indeterminately from anything in itself. If passing events must, to some extent, be referred to former influence, still even this is apt to be found in outward circumstances. A constitution, an ordered working from certain established principles and under certain conditions, is unwillingly admitted. Now, not to speak of the difficulty of conceiving anything as not being constructed with definite elements and parts related to each other and the whole, so as to determine more or less its procedures, the evidence that society has a structure, is overwhelming. In reviewing the past an immense amount of human history is plainly seen to have been the result of inward forces and tendencies, certain to work under their correspondent conditions in just the way they did. So that in looking into the future, one may confidently anticipate a vast amount of human activities and states from well ascertained existence and course of elements in society. The individual man has no more proved himself to have a structure upon which may be based certain consequences, than has society shown itself to be an organic system whose constitution may be studied. For indeed, humanity, as beheld in society, irresistibly makes the impression of being something more than individual men coming together by agreement or accident. Doubtless men are personal in the fullest sense conceivable. They have a range of arbitrariness in which they originate and arrange and consciously determine to an unknown extent. The sphere in which this will is freely exercised, though never consciously invaded, is yet included in an immense continuous unity of human being, of which it is a living part. The exact relation of this unity to the individual may not be defined, but it is impossible to account for many phenomena of good and evil in men's lives, without recognizing their determination in part, by that unity acting through the family and race. The scriptures make this prominent. Indeed, men object to the ancient revelation on this account, but their objections apply equally to what nature teaches, for there the evidence is of the most various and strongest kind—that history proceeds more or less in solidarity—anticipating much for the individual emerging from it. So no matter what difficulties men find with this as a theological article of belief, it sturdily remains to be considered as a fact in nature, the absence of which cannot even be conceived of without disturbing the identity of man. But if, on the one hand, this unity determines in a measure the individual; on the other, the individual consciously or unconsciously anticipates for the future of others and determines, in a measure, that very unity to which he is related. Now, what is this other than the vicarious element? a mode of existence and development in which race and nation and family have represented and acted for the individual, while in turn the individual has represented and acted for the race and nation, and family. This vicarious working is found everywhere and always in the greatest variety of forms and degrees, and belongs to the innermost social structure of man. If now, we confine our view to individuals, and find that even where there is the most distinct individuality and the most personal absoluteness conceivable, yet such a relation exists between individuals that they affect each other to the extent of acting for and being identified with each other, and this for good or evil, and further, that this mode of the relation is universal and constant, so that men cannot make it cease but only vary its direction, what other conclusion is there than that human society is so constructed. It is well at this point to remark, that if any objections are offered to one occurrence of the vicarious, they apply logically to all such occurrences for good as for evil, and then, finally the difficulty will be with the structure of society itself. But it would be hard to show how humanity could be constituted in society without the vicarious. All this has been considered irrespective of the moral character which human nature might have. Some such character it must have, but whether good or evil, the constituted being in which this good or evil would be found, would remain the same. The tremendous event of sin is, after all, as regards the structure of human nature, only an incident. True, we cannot exaggerate the evil of sin, but actually it is a perversion of human nature's powers and modes by a self, alienated from God and centered in itself.

This sinful self misuses these powers and modes, but it must use them, for it has nothing else to use. Moral evil cannot introduce any new power or mode into human nature, nor can it destroy any. It has no need, for the utmost alienation from God and discord with men can be seen to be perversions of existing powers, and the penalties for such perversions all proceed in constitutional modes. But more than this: there is hardly any limit to the scope afforded by these powers and modes. Human sin might go far beyond anything yet known, in debasement and exaggeration of self, and still be manifested only in the misuse of nature. On the other hand, if moral good alone characterized human nature, its relation to the structure of this nature and its modes of development, would be the same as that of moral evil. It would use them. True, we cannot conceive of the difference between such use and the present misuse. Our highest moral conception could not be equal to what must be the effect of the human self entirely centered in God and accordant with fellow beings. But even this would, in fact, be only the right use of human nature's powers and modes. Such a holy self must use them, for it too, would have nothing else to use. Moral good cannot introduce any new power or mode into human nature nor can it destroy any. Here, too, there is no need, for when we imagine universal and perfect goodness its illustrations will be the right use of this same structure of human nature; and so in parallel opposite to the supposition of evil, there is no conceivable limit to the scope for moral good afforded by these powers and modes of development. The utmost human goodness could not manifest itself in any other way. If then the vicarious is a mode of development which belongs to the structure of society, so that human nature in its social life and activity must use this mode whether for good or evil, then we may look for it on all sides in the actual history of man. We begin with the most fundamental instance and the largest scale, and where the least will and consciousness are concerned.

The vicarious in representativeness. And first, representativeness in race. Universal history warrants very positive conclusions respecting the relation of our earliest race to all who have proceeded from it. It is a relation in which the preceding determines more or less what follows. We need not measure the exact extent of this. Nor is it necessary to mark the limits of individuality. Enough now to observe, of the race, that its past is so uniform in this determination of the future as to form the ground largely of history. Education in great part, and much providing for the affairs of men, assume that it is an essential mode in the life of the race. But this involves the vicarious. If man before, no matter where beginning, does to any extent determine man following, so far he acts for him, and represents him. But we can observe nearer, this representativeness in the sub-races. It is certainly within bounds to affirm that whenever the type of any one of the various divisions of mankind came to be, that type has remained essentially the same for longer or shorter periods and perhaps has never wholly disappeared. Thus the Negro and Mongolian illustrate how a type may continue. If there be modifications, these, too, tend to repeat themselves. The Aryan has divided into different varieties and undergone the greatest modifications, and still certain characteristics of the parent stock are preserved, while the modifications themselves now distinguishing modern nationalities from one another and their common Aryan ancestors, have maintained themselves with great persistency. Now here in circumstances of endless diversity and with consequences of incalculable moment, making history of vastest extent, representativeness constantly appears. Men act for those who come after. More or less they determine for their descendants, and this is the more instructive for our study, that this representativeness works more or less independently of men's intentions or even consciousness. Now here we have in the divine government a constitution of human society which has for one of its modes of development the vicarious, and this particular form, representativeness, is seen on examination to have prevailed from the first. We have looked at it on the largest scale. Beyond any question the mode of acting for, representing, characterizes human development in the race at large, and in each division of the race we shall find the same repeated on a smaller scale. At this point it may be worth while to consider some things already suggested by our study. Whatever difficulties are found with the teachings of Revelation concerning human nature in its social relations, are met equally in the actual history of man, for this shows in the clearest manner that humanity exists in unity of race, and that this unity, to a certain extent, anticipates and determines for the individuals proceeding from it. So the preceding act for and represent those who come after. If a difficulty is found with this, in relation to moral evil and its consequences, the same exists in relation to moral good and its consequences. For we have studied human nature as a structure irrespective of moral contents, and have seen that it has an inherent mode of existence and development to be used by either good or evil. If there be difficulty about being individually sinful, so is there about being individually good, and then about being individually moral at all, and finally about individuality itself. But though we cannot fix the limits of individuality, yet we recognize at once an individual and are as sure of his being such, as we can be of anything. Indeed, this is fundamental. But we are certain too, of human unity. Even though we cannot conciliate the two, yet we must believe both and keep them in view, else the course of events as well as personal characteristics and conduct were unintelligible, as they would be impossible without human unity and human individuality existing together. So then we accept both without weakening either. It may be that in studying their various relations we shall find much in harmony with the fullest doctrine of a Saviour's redemption.

The Vicarious in the Family and Nation.

WE will next consider the vicarious element as it appears in the family. This belongs to the same category with race, and on a smaller scale presents more strikingly the same phenomena. The importance of the family to a complete view of man, of course is admitted. At the outset one thing is to be noticed. In the matter of belonging to race, choice is in no way concerned. But will is involved in the beginning of family life. When, however, the family has once been constituted, there is no choice as to some of the modes in which that life must proceed. That which we are considering, the vicarious, is a necessity of family life. As in the race, so in the family, there are types. Some families have them more marked than others, but all have them. Physical characteristics are continued to a certain extent and some features reappear for generations. No less distinguishable is the recurrence of mental peculiarities in the family. This is so common as to excite no surprise. If it be said genius is seldom repeated in the same family, or even eminent talent, yet this occurs often enough for the point in question. Even where the greatest unlikeness prevails, it is not difficult to discover something of a family type. But more important in our study, is the question of moral peculiarities being continued. Of course, we cannot exactly tell where the moral quality begins, or its degree, nor is this other than might be expected in man as he actually is. But it may be affirmed with confidence that moral evil, within certain limits, appears in families under typical forms.

While at ground sin must be the same in all, self centered in self, particular sinful tendencies and habits characterize one family in distinction from another, and these may repeat themselves in successive generations. So, too, certain fine qualities plainly appear to be transmitted. Thus, without extravagance, and after due allowance for education and all surrounding circumstances, we confidently may distinguish family excellencies and family sins. Now here, affecting us much more noticeably, is the same fact, which we observed in the race at large. Here is the same determining for the future of others, representing and acting for them. The more closely we follow the course of family life, the more we are struck with its vicarious working for good and evil. A large part of family history is of parents acting representatively for children without intelligent purpose. A large part, however, of representativeness in the family is attended with consciousness and will. The parent acts intelligently for the child and represents him in affairs of the greatest moment. The daily course of life furnishes instances of willing vicarious action. Human statutes recognize it substantially. The rite of infant baptism has its natural ground in this representativeness. It assumes that the parent may promise for the child, since whether he promise or not, he certainly will, to an immense extent, act for and determine the child in the direction of good or evil, and his choice is only between the two alternatives. In many cases the happiness and suffering of the family come vicariously, come not on account of the persons enjoying or suffering, but for another. Often this is so great in degree as to amount to substitution. The parent in place of the child, the child in place of the parent. Within the sphere of home an almost identification of persons is formed through the working of natural affection. Again, the character which is to be in one is more or less involved in another, and will more or less depend for what it shall be upon what the other is. The ancient scripture is full of illustrations of the vicarious element in the family. Thus it commands parents to act for their children, taking for granted that parents represented and could act for them. A remarkable recognition of this is seen in the famous declaration of the warrior judge of the Hebrews, "As for me and my house we will serve the Lord." This is certainly very strong but it is not distinguished except in the degree of consciousness, from many other instances in scripture where the vicarious element is recognized. The Jewish history, as seen in Revelation, continually presents this mode of development in family life, for good and evil. But all history records the same divine government as that which is described by inspiration. Of course, then, the objections brought against Revelation in respect to the vicarious element in the family, apply equally to its appearance in all history. If the question of the individual again comes up, the same is to be said as in the matter of race; unquestionably metaphysical difficulties will remain here as there. But practically no more difficulty exists in the immediate relation of the family, than in the seemingly more remote one of race. In both relations, the individual exists with undiminished personality. In family life, then, where we are most intimately concerned, we find that the vicarious is a necessary mode of development.

II. National life is too important not to be considered in this connection. Indeed the nation bears a large part in human development. We see plainly the divine intent to gather men into nations, and through them to carry on its designs. Thus in Revelation we have a record of wonderful training, by which the Jews were to be formed into a nation. We can follow them through their nomadic state; their settlement in Egypt; their conflicts in Palestine, and their subjection to a system of laws remarkably adapted to promote an intense national life. In order to keep moral truths of vital importance to the world, and bear them through the ages, it was necessary that there should be a nation, apart, with the most pronounced national consciousness. To fulfill their grand mission, the Jews had a most peculiar discipline, but they perverted this as they did other things, and failed to preserve a complete national existence. But what the Jews did fulfill of the mission assigned them, has been the unspeakable blessing of mankind, and illustrates the importance of the nation in the world economy. Other histories, ancient and modern, confirm this view. The ground instinct in our late struggle, was to preserve our national life. In every community two opposing forces, integrating and disintegrating, come in conflict, and on the issue turns the question whether or not there shall be a nation. But when at last a real nation has come to be, it has a unity of its own. It is possessed of an organic life. A national sentiment is formed. National characteristics appear over and above those of race. There is a national consciousness which can be appealed to and acts vigorously. Now, in this great form of society, where so much of human history is embodied, representativeness prevails. The men of one time in this national life, act for those of another to all intents, as if they stood in their place. They determine for them nationally. Their counsels, their actions, often their sufferings; are, in large part, for those who are to come after. Nay, in one sense, they are more for others than for themselves. Thus, frequently in the history of the chosen people, they are reminded that upon the conduct of those then addressed, depends the destiny of those who shall follow them. It is impressed upon them that they choose not for themselves only, but for their descendants. God is revealed as dealing with them in successive periods, concerning the future represented by them. Recall, for example, the explicit declaration made to them when they enter upon their inheritance, that they and their posterity were connected in the closest manner, so that their present and immediately following times, were to have a very great influence upon the future, and that in fact they represented a coming national life of immense interest to the world. The idea of acting for others was so variously and forcibly inculcated, that this vicarious relation found expression in moments of deep feeling, not indeed showing the people's appreciation of its full significance, but proving the instruction they had received on this point.

An illustration of the profound incorporation of this idea into the Jewish mind, may be seen when in their fearful rejection of Christ, the frenzied hierarchy uttered those words of horror, "His blood be upon us and our children!" In that dreadful challenge to the divine Nemesis, the most impressive meaning is derived from the principle we are studying. It was no idle word then uttered. The actors in that national sin included with themselves their children, by no fiction of rage, but they accepted the responsibility, which really existed, of representing them, and actual history tells in Israel's after sins and woes, how fatal was that representation. Jewish history was selected for an instance because it is an inspired record, and the occasion was so momentous. But the history of any nation will afford illustrations. Select some marked period. Not that such was different, except in degree of importance from others. It is easy to see how, at that period, men were acting consciously or unconsciously, for those who were to come after. Thus, at various times decisions were made which involved the destinies of millions yet to be born. The ages succeeding the fall of Rome, apparently so confused, will be found remarkably full of what may be termed representative events. But we have illustrations nearer our own days, which are still more striking. The French Revolution seems at first, an almost unlimited arbitrariness of human acts, but really there were antecedents of tremendous potency in the preceding century, and the men of that period, to an extent which it is difficult to measure, did determine what their descendants should suffer and be. So, too, in the change which the study of history has undergone, England is now regarded more in the connections of its successive periods. This, to us, is especially interesting, for we can find not a little of our own present determined for us generations ago. It is not difficult to fix upon particular times, which were representative in a remarkable degree, when men were settling questions, of even greater moment for those to come after, than for themselves, and were more or less conscious of this. Surely the early times of our own history were highly representative. The men of those days did act for us very largely, and determine our subsequent history. So the conduct of the generation at the Revolution, decided whether or no we should develop into a republic. Some of the men in that day were very conscious of this, but though feeling great responsibility, they had no misgivings about determining for their posterity. They represented us to an almost unlimited extent, and we were born into their conclusions. We were not consulted about it, and so far from perpetually renewing our consent to be what we were born, we resisted with the whole force of the nation, the attempt to undo our fathers' work for us. The horrors of that secession strife, met with intelligent purpose and willing action, were our testimony to all time, that we accepted our ancestors' transactions as for us. It was a great moment in our history, and even now we do not appreciate its full significance. And still, though with less exciting events, and less concentration of opposing forces, and less appearance of momentous consequences, this same mode of development goes on and we are acting for those who shall come after us. We represent them. Thus God governs: not by surface agitation of individuals, not by pure arbitrariness of men in the present, but largely by representativeness in the past, of a nation's unity. We know nothing of other intelligent beings than man, and can only conjecture concerning them, that they are purely individual. But a great peculiarity of man is that which we have dwelt upon. Within a certain scope, he has an entirely separate life. He is a conscious person, and has a will capable of different possibilities. Like our conception of higher intelligences, he is a completely discriminated self, but unlike what we think them to be, he has, so to speak, roots, a substantial part in a unity with others. This we have all along treated as the ground of the phenomena observed. Real history has respect to this unity, giving centuries to truths and energies which cannot be bounded by the lives of individuals, that are offshoots from the great out-spreading vine—waves and eddies in the majestic current of humanity. Now, this being recognized, it will be found that among the methods by which this unity produces great results, representativeness is very prominent. It may be said to mediate between the past and future. It is the recipient of the national life and contains its concentrated expression. The past is indeed irrevocable. Whatever has been done for us, whatever we have done up to our instant, is actual, and God's judgment is fixed upon us, and them who, years since, helped to make us. In this sense representativeness mirrors and judges a certain past. In relation to the future, it anticipates within a range of possibilities, the characters and events to come. By it Providence brings into the present, as if in a qualified sense of prophecy, the things that shall be, and gives men, within limits, the sublime power to determine the lot of their descendants. On the one hand, this unity assures us in history, that the destiny of a country is not left to human extemporaneousness. On the other it is in the power of existing men, at all times, even in matters of greatest historical importance, to shape the future, in large degree. Thus has been brought fully into view, a mode of human development. We have found it prevailing alike in the histories of the race, of the sub-races, of families and of nations. If again, the question comes up of the individual's substantial personality, his conscious self, his freedom of action, his power over his own opinions and character, as in relation to a unity in the past, it is to be observed, in the first place, that we have nothing to do with this. Our one enquiry is as to the fact and extent of the vicarious element in the structure and development of humanity. Still we may repeat, that any difficulties which may be found, apply to all parts of the system in which we are. Nay, more, they will apply to any system that can be conceived of, where actual man should exist. In the second place, man is all the individual we can imagine him to be. Here, as elsewhere, we cannot conciliate truths which are equally established. The conciliation lies in a plane far above us, if not above all finite being. Enough for us, that made in the image of God, possessed of a conscious personality which, sin, no more than holiness, can affect, we may reverently study our nature and its modes.

The Vicarious in Natural Affections.

IN GENERAL INTERCOURSE ; IN LITERATURE ; IN RELATION TO NATURAL LAW.

THE natural affections have much to do with the development of human nature. Their strength and purity signify largely the good estate of society. Their weakness and corruption mark surely human degradation. They afford channels for moral character, though not in themselves moral character. Hence, they are all the more striking illustrations of the vicarious. They are exercised more or less vicariously, of necessity. The selfishness or unselfishness of the person exercising them, need not be considered : even the happiness or unhappiness which they minister makes no difference. It is safe to state, generally, that men, in the natural course of these instinctive feelings towards their fellow creatures, do bear in themselves, much of what belongs to others. Thus in the relation which is the beginning of human society, the truer the union, the more there is of reciprocal assumption. Much of this is intelligent choice ; the willing taking upon self, what is anothers. When we have admired some act of wifely devotion, some long continued endurance, and have spoken of the costly sacrifice, we were not careful to note, that by the necessary working of this structure of humanity, what appeared to us so lovely, was by the vicarious mode which we are studying. Again, in many instances, persons bound by ties of kindred, are drawn into vortices of misery by no will of their own. The substitution was involuntary, sometimes, indeed, unwillingly endured, but at others accepted. Not seldom in the unwritten tragedies of life, we see the keenest anguish endured, not by the selfish voluptuary, not by the unfeeling dishonest, but by pure and honorable spirits, who, bound as living to the dead, cannot escape the dreadful unity. So frequent is this in our actual system, that when we look on some character possessed of a peculiar moral intelligence and chastened grace, we are never surprised to hear of its daily suffering for others. Nay, so remarkable is this chapter of human nature, that sometimes we feel the only possibility for certain heartless souls to be roused to moral sensibility, would be to have their destiny linked with more exalted natures, who should be smitten to death in the fellowship of their shame, yes, sometimes in this wondrous world, the good perish that the wicked may live, and men have knelt by graves which their own sins have dug. But the mother's relation to the child affords the climax of the vicarious element in the sphere of natural affection. Here the identifying of self with another, is something wonderful. The mother lives, as it were, the life of the child. Here is capacity for any amount of vicarious joy or pain. Affection cannot express itself to the utmost, without assuming thus another, almost to identity. What instances of this come up to every mind! How much of earth's happiness and misery is due to the necessity of a mother's love, manifesting itself vicariously. Who can measure the sin and mischief in our world, where this affection, and its mode of expression, are directed and impelled by a thoroughly worldly character! Who shall tell the blessed histories of good, wrought by this loveliest and strongest of all instinctive affections, when exercised by high moral natures. How, in some instances, has every other tie seemed to give way, and yet the conviction of a mother's love has proved strong enough to stay the course of selfish passion. This relation affords the most striking illustration, but the same mode is more or less apparent, through the whole range of what are termed natural affections. If these comprehend feeling to country, a wide field of observation opens. Here are found many of the noblest and basest deeds and lives of history. Now it is very strikingly evident, that men, in this relation, live and act under a necessity of vicarious action. They may choose deliberately ; they may follow an impulse, but the mode of their acting is already settled for them. They do not originate it; they cannot change it. A mighty ruler—a petty actor in village concerns—a beneficent statesman—a mischevious politician—a patriot—a traitor—though their motives be as wide apart as the poles, must alike use the same mode. They must proceed vicariously. They cannot act for themselves alone. Be their devotion to country surpassingly great—be their lust for selfish power monstrous, be the most various good or numerous evils, the result of their opposite actions, they have alike put themselves in the place of others—acted for them. Thus, if we have studied aright, it is found, that even the natural affections, in the whole extent of their relations, come under the same condition, and cannot be conducted for good or ill, except more or less in the vicarious mode. True, none fully make this tremendous condition real to themselves, or clearly see that they do not and cannot live their own life alone, but that all the time they are

acting for others. On the contrary, they try to persuade
themselves, and are largely persuaded, that their life is
wholly individual. But this is only part of the great lie.
The scheme of our existence is the farthest possible from it.

II. The vicarious in general intercourse. We have already had much of human intercourse in view, but if we would make our study exhaustive, there is much remaining to confirm our observations. Thus international affairs, in which questions of greatest importance, such as peace and commerce, are treated, afford additional examples. Men cannot proceed here, except vicariously. According to the weightiness of the matter, is the dignity of the person sent as representative, and he stands in place of his nation, with great powers to act for it. This mode is nothing extraordinary. Indeed, there is no other mode possible, and no one finds the least difficulty in accepting it. Yet here is the vicarious element on the largest scale, and often involving consequences of greatest moment. Even more striking is the vicarious in government itself. Every form of this must be a representation of the governed by the governing. Really there can be nothing less. Government is no more a necessity, than being acted for. The loosest democracy is no more independent individualism at last, than the closest autocracy. Millions depend in matters of property and life, and character, on the government acting for them, and there is no other way. If, now, we examine the course of affairs in more private life, as in the transaction of business, it will be found that in the sphere of property, this same mode of vicarious action is employed to an amazing extent, and by an unmistakable necessity. Not merely in vastest and most distant concerns of commerce, but in smallest matters, and right before us, all the time, are taking place vicarious acts. Here are assumptions of others, liabilities and sureties given, and acts for others, and substitutions of self for others. Then, too, the interests involved, and the consequences following, are often exceeding great. Not merely material loss or gain, but human happiness and character are largely concerned. Certainly the prevalence of the vicarious element in this part of human activity, ought to have great significance, for it is not arbitrarily chosen, but employed of necessity. Men cannot transact these affairs without acting vicariously. It were not difficult to trace the working of the same mode, in other parts of human intercourse. Even in commonest contacts, men are doing or enjoying or suffering for others. Sometimes we shudder at the malevolent use of the vicarious element, when an intelligent selfishness controls the soul. Often the feeling of discouragement arises at the proportion of apparent unconsciousness of vicarious selfishness on the part of men. On the other hand, we can see benevolence employing the vicarious element, for purposes of good, and the more that unselfish souls are found in the activities of love, the more frequent is the use of this mode to promote human welfare. Very striking, too, and pointing on to what we aim at in our study, is the fact, that as benevolence itself deepens and widens, and the benefit to be wrought grows larger, and its difficulties come more into view, so the vicarious element to be used, assumes larger proportions. More emptying of self and assumption of others, and identification with them, to increased extent of loss and suffering, will, of necessity, present themselves. Doubtless this is the way in which God trains men, and leads them to conquest over evil. They do not see at first what

is demanded of them, else they might recoil. It is when
their hearts are more engaged in the work, and their benevolence is more rooted, and their moral sense more luminously strong, and their wills have become more fixed towards God, that the work itself shows its true dimensions,
and the condition of its success. Certainly it is in accepting this condition, that individual characters prove the
soundness of their moral substance. On the other hand,
who can doubt that it is the sight of this necessary mode of
benevolent action, the more or less distinct impression of
what it involves, which alarms our selfishness and keeps us
to our low moral averages. If we have observed truly,
then, not only here and there in human life shall we find the
vicarious element, but wherever men act in relation to each
other. They cannot associate without fulfilling, for good or
evil, some necessity of the vicarious mode.

III. It is no slight confirmation of the preceding to find
it recognized in human literature. And this is important
testimony, because letters are the expression of human nature. The most creative imagination is limited by the ma-
terials out of which its forms come, and one characteristic
of highest genius is, that it deals with what is fundamental
in human nature. No scholar needs to be reminded that
the chief tragedies of the ancients—never surpassed, if ever
equalled—largely employ the vicarious in their very ground
structure. But in modern works which aim to describe the
most inward and profoundest working of human nature, it is
curious to observe how the vicarious with various degrees of
fullness is employed as the mode of development for characters and events. And this is done not only without apparent consciousness of any thing unnatural, but with the evi-

dent conviction that these instances of vicarious action are perfectly natural. At times, too, this is by writers very far from sympathy with the vicarious element in redemption. As, for example, two noted authors of our day. One is French; he distinctly rejects Revelation. His enormous egoism glares and reaches out its feelers like his huge cuttle fish. This writer employs the vicarious mode in its fullest sense, confident that he has written nothing discordant with the course of nature. The other is English, doubtless more orthodox than the Frenchman, yet there is little to choose between them, morally. This author, too, makes use of the extremest form of the vicarious, that of substitution, to be the crowning act in his work. And he also was sure, that this would carry the assent of his readers, that though a wonderful climax of self-devotion, it yet illustrated in the completest form, what is actual. It will be found that modern literature has a very full recognition of the vicarious in nature. So that, though men may refuse to receive a Saviour whose redemption has a vicarious element, yet they cannot deny the existence of the vicarious, nor object to Christ for that. Strange comment is it on human thought, that when a theologian ended his treatise with the denial of a vicarious Redeemer, as if nature were against such, a poet of his age and nation, makes the idea and beauty of his drama out of the vicarious mode in nature. As well may men expel the bow of God from Creation. Though the molten sky has not a cloud to mirror it, the dash of the mountain torrent, the spray of a tiny rivulet, shall give forth the same form as that of the mightier arch.

IV. Natural law, in the relation to the vicarious, has, in part, been anticipated, since natural law is, of course, concerned in human nature. But here are meant the forces of physical nature, external to man, with which he is constantly in contact, and his harmony or discord with which, affects his whole course. These laws confirm the statement that we live in a vicarious system. They work in correspondence with the various forms of the vicarious, which we have considered. In our day, men are giving great attention to what are termed "The laws of society." Now these laws, by their quiet resistless action, teach as really as by voice, that men are so related to each other, as in a very full sense, to be "their brothers' keepers." So by fixed results, these laws confirm "solidarity, representativeness, substitution," for good and evil. This is coming out to view very strikingly— men are finding that they cannot be safe nor sound socially, while they are selfishly individual and independent, and that the attempt to be so in the past, has been largely the occasion of human crimes and miseries. Thus men are coming to hear such laws utter more articulately—"Man must live in and for his fellow"—with all the logical conclusions that follow. But, as already seen, this involves vicarious living and acting, to indefinite extent. Over against all, waits natural law to enforce the mode, and there is no evading that law. Thus, when men seek in the storm to rescue an imperiled crew, law is there to exact vicarious peril. So in time of pestilence, when benevolent hearts recognize the claim of brotherhood, law is present to enforce vicarious action. Again, in every effort to remove some great evil, when one might even wish for relaxation of the condition, as the evil shows itself more difficult to be removed, natural law seems more impressively present and fixed than ever, and insists on costlier use of the vicarious mode. One thing may be noticed here in advance of its later application. However men may object to the vicarious element in redemption, they are never offended with any extent of vicarious suffering by man, when it is willingly endured for others. On the contrary, the extremest instances of substitution, in which property, and every earthly good, and life itself, are freely given up for others, excite the highest moral approval of mankind. They are carefully recorded, and looked upon as bright spots in our dark wastes of selfishness. Nay, men, incapable of such actions themselves, are impatient with others when, on some great emergency, they fail to put themselves in the place of those exposed to peril. Even in common life, who does not accept various substitutions of others for himself, without objection. How many services rendered and kind acts performed, employ this mode, and no one finds fault with it. Thus the attempt has been made to study the vicarious in nature. If we have observed correctly, it has been found not to be an extraordinary or occasional appearance, not to be originated by man even in some remarkable circumstances. But it is seen to be in the very structure of society, and to be an essential mode in human development. It has been manifest in race and sub-race, in family and nation, in natural affections and general intercourse, and in literature, and we have seen how it was enforced by natural law. In fact, we have found it wherever man is related to man. Consciously or unconsciously, man has acted in this mode. Good and evil have been administered vicariously, so that we cannot conceive of human nature without it. Hence, if any new doom were to come on man, we could not help expecting it would work in some way vicariously. On the other hand, if any good, however exalted, should be manifested to man, can we think of it in this actual system, as not in some way recognizing the vicarious mode, since a mighty pedagogy of nature has led us to anticipate this? And so, if some magnificent work of help should come, and men should object to a vicarious element in it, they must also object to this actual human nature.

Moral Good and Evil Manifested in Human Nature, of Necessity Vicariously.

THE CONSEQUENCES OF GOOD AND EVIL IN RELATION TO THE VICARIOUS. THE VICARIOUS IN HUMAN EFFORTS TO ESCAPE CONSEQUENCES OF EVIL..

WE have considered the vicarious in the structure of human nature, as a mode of its development irrespective of moral character. If such a conception seem difficult, since actual human nature is moral, yet no more difficulty is involved, than in considering, by itself, any thing else belonging to human nature which is not necessarily dependent on moral character. It might be shown, too, that in our world system, below man, where no moral is found, something corresponding to our vicarious action appears. But at all events, our humanity affords not the least evidence that a vicarious mode originated after any moral period, or first appeared on the occurrence of new outward surroundings. So we may conclude that moral good or evil, whichever may be the character of human nature, must manifest and develop itself vicariously. So to speak, it finds this mode just as it finds other modes, and must use it. The human will—however free and personal—choosing to be and do good or evil, must yet act vicariously in its existing relation to others. Hence, in advance, we may affirm of the great matter of human character, be it what it may, or become what it will, that throughout its course to any completeness, good or evil, possible in our world, it must proceed in this mode, and we can form some conception of what would be the state of things, if moral good entirely possessed humanity. It is not difficult to imagine, how such goodness, existing and acting vicariously, in persons related to each other, would produce a society, just the opposite of what now is. When we see how evil uses the vicarious mode, and representation and substitution are forms of the mode in which selfish man inflicts untold injury upon his fellow, and then think of the entire contrary to all this, we are prepared for a very noble conception of human nature. For try to think of the vicarious in all its degrees of fullness, and throughout its vast extent of use, employed only to bless men. Imagine human nature perfectly holy. Self entirely subject to God; every affection centered in him; no such consciousness of self as admits of an end apart from him. A will coincident with the divine, and knowing not an eddy of volition against the majestic flow of infinite Providence. Then consider what must follow in the moral order stated by our Lord, that such a self would be in perfect harmony with fellow beings, loving others as self, rejoicing in their happiness, complacent in their goodness, seeking their every possible advantage. All this is legitimate thought. If now we think of such human nature manifesting itself in action to men, we must conceive of it as employing this vicarious mode. Then what a view opens to us. The vicarious in the race and sub-race, the family, the nation, and in all social intercourse, would be prevalent, as now, but it would be only as a method of benevolence. Simply following out this idea, what possibilities of moral good would be afforded in the exercise of this method. What visions of vicarious love rise before the mind! And if this be thought mere imagination, yet be it remembered, that so far as moral good acts in our world, it employs this mode largely, as we have already seen. If now the vicarious element appeared only as it was used by a human nature without moral evil, it is very doubtful if any objections would be offered, and yet, logically, there should be. On the other hand, in considering the possibilities of moral evil in our world, we go over the same ground. If we imagine human wickedness as far exceeding what we have known, and exhaust our power of conceiving the selfishness that could be exercised by man, it will be found that we at once think of it as employing a vicarious mode in which to develop. Thus it would manifest itself in race, and sub-race, and family, and nation, and all social intercourse. Here, too, we have the use which, moral evil has actually made of this mode, and hence are only completing, in thought, what is already actual. Objections to evil, working thus, cannot be considered alone, but, as seen above, must apply equally, if at all, to moral good work, in the same way. If fairly considered then, we conclude that the vicarious mode belongs to the structure of humanity, in which moral character has its being, but is independent of that moral character, and is certain to be used by it, whether good or evil, just as other things belong to the structure of humanity, irrespective of its moral character. So it is not difficult to see, that man's moral character may change from good to evil, and from evil to good, yet these changes take place without in the least affecting the vicarious element, which has no moral quality to be changed and which remains the same, and is used only as a mode. Hence we are safe in affirming, that moral good and evil, in our world, are, of necessity, to a great extent, manifested vicariously.

II. The consequences of good and evil considered in relation to the vicarious in nature. Moral good and evil may well be expected to be attended with gravest consequences. For moral character must be more important than anything else. To admit something superior, or even equal to right, is to deny its existence. We must believe God so regards what concerns moral issues in his government. Himself infinitely holy, he must exalt righteousness and honor his own law. To him moral evil must be abhorrent The one involves the other. If he makes himself known, this must appear. To conceive of God as indifferent whether there be good or evil, and whether no consequences follow either, or the same consequences both, is to deny God. Hence we cannot be surprised, if God so orders the universe, that results of vastest moment depend upon moral character. We should be surprised if it were not so. Sometimes, indeed, it is denied that moral character has any discriminating effect on events, but oftener it is alleged that much moral confusion exists from the want of perfect discrimination. Now not to dwell on this world being probationary and educational, and so requiring mixed issues, it is admitted that human society presents many dark problems, felt to be such by observers in every age. Still, it cannot be gainsayed, that history shows the well or ill-being of society to be inseparably connected with moral good or evil. So that we are fully warranted in believing that the greatest conceivable well-being would follow perfect goodness in our system, and a proportionate ill-being would follow completed wickedness. For think again of human nature as entirely sound, morally, supreme love to God and equal love to man. Recall the necessary conception of self, in a normal state. Then follow out, in all possible relations, the action of such moral good. At once arises, of necessity, a view of human well-being. Every thing which would be of highest advantage to the community, and the individual, immediately occurs to the mind. There is no motive for anything else. Such benevolence can only lead to harmony of wills, and universal blessedness. On the other hand, carry out as before the conception of human wickedness. Imagine the alienation from God greater—the separation from man wider—think of self more exaggerated, and so of selfishness more intense, and comprehensive, till we cannot go farther in thought of man's sinfulness; every step of this dreary way will be accompanied by a picture of human wretchedness. This is our necessary thought, and history educates us, even in this mixed state, to expect that consequences will follow character. How, indeed, can any look out on life, and not feel that the greatest argument is going on all the time for the good and against the bad. The whole of man's existence on earth, so far as we know it, is a witness for the moral law. Indeed, our life is a hopeless enigma, unless we recognize a divine expression of moral distinction. Now these consequences, in such connections, occurring in our system, will be found very largely vicarious in their mode. Thus happiness is on account of others character, to an immense extent. The view taken already of representativeness, includes this. As character itself is more or less affected for good by the conduct of progenitors, who acted for their descendants, so, in large part, are blessings enjoyed by these descendants, the consequences of that conduct. It is delightful to trace much of one's present happiness to those who acted for us. We can plainly see the results of our ancestors' virtues in the advantages of our political and social state. But more particularly in family histories we can follow the consequences of moral good, working vicariously. Who can measure the obligation of children to the character of their parents, for what they enjoy. The scriptures declare that often for the parents sake, calamity is averted from a family, and its welfare assured. Certainly there is much in actual observation to agree with this, and the view may be extended indefinitely. On every side, and in various ways, we see men possessed of advantages, which are the consequences of good in others. If this be questioned, the answer again is the structure of human nature whereby the individual is closely related to the whole, or parts of the whole. Questioning this, is questioning human nature itself. Besides it is not likely men would make any question, if only happy consequences were concerned. But, of course, there is another side to be considered. If now we observe the working of the consequences of evil, the same vicarious element will be found. The scriptures declare in the clearest manner, that men suffer the consequences of others sins. History and observation make this palpable. On the largest scale it is seen in races and sub-races. The wickedness of remote progenitors, bears fruit in disastrous consequences, continuing through generations. In families the dark side of this mode, in the administration of consequences, furnishes the saddest tragedies of earth. Already in illustration of part of our subject reference has been made to the suffering of parents on account of the misconduct of children. But there is a wider scope and more fearful aspect to the sufferings of children, in consequence of the sins of parents. It is impossible to ignore this, earth is full of it. Here are families enduring every variety of ill, because the heads of those families were wicked and foolish. In whatever direction we turn our eyes, we shall see the consequences of moral evil. Society appears full of finest reticulations, uniting men, and render it impossible for them not to affect one another vicariously, and hence, if the bad consequences of moral evil work in such a system, they must, more or less, work vicariously. Of course it must be kept in mind that moral evil is true of all, that no one suffers in this world who is wholly free from sin. Still men do suffer from the consequences of sins, in respect to which they are relatively innocent. It is here that the greatest difficulties are met. Every one must admit the painful force of the questions which arise. But we must always keep in mind that objections to the vicarious, in consequences of evil, logically involve objections to the vicarious in consequences of good. We cannot see how this mode can be employed for human happiness, without the other alternative. And if we resolutely object to the vicarious in consequences, at all, we must to any vicarious element, and that is objecting to the actual structure of humanity. But that ends the whole matter.

III. It yet remains, in order to complete our view, that we notice how man makes "use of the vicarious in his efforts to avoid the consequences of sin." This, too, is within the domain of actual human nature, and part of the "earthly things" discriminated by our Lord. However great man's moral insensibility may become, he can hardly ever be without some apprehension of the guilt of sin. With different degrees of intelligence, this feeling is apparent everywhere in the history of man. Now if what we have observed of the prevalence of the vicarious in nature, be true, we might expect, that in a matter so important as deliverance from the penalty of sin, the vicarious would appear in man's efforts to be delivered. And this is just what does appear, in one form or another, to an immense extent. One cannot read the history of religions, without being struck by the use which is made of the vicarious, on the human side, towards the objects of the feelings of guilt and fear. It is very superficially said, that priests originate these feelings, and the vicarious direction taken by them. Priests may, indeed, exaggerate and use for selfish ends, such feelings and modes, but they cannot originate that of which they are part. They themselves are originated as a class, in the working of these feelings. Nor can they be accounted for otherwise. So that we cannot avoid the conclusion, that the vicarious in men's efforts to escape the consequences of sin, is also perfectly natural.

Thus have we gone over a field full of important bearings on the great doctrine of christianity. It is well to study what is natural, for the better apprehension of the supernatural. This is in the order of truth, marked out by our Lord himself. It may be, there is need of abatement in some things which have been stated, but upon the whole, we may conclude that the vicarious in varying forms, but at ground one, is a mode, not coming into use at a particular time, or in certain circumstances, or only in some human relations, or as something which could be dispensed with. Far from this, it appears at first, and always since, under the greatest variety of circumstances. We have seen it in the very structure of human nature, and thence in human development. We have studied it in the race and sub-race, in the family and nation, in natural affections, and general intercourse of men. We have observed the working of physical laws in regard to it. We have seen it recognized in letters. So we found it independent of the personal will, and remarked how it existed, and was used alike in the working of moral good, or evil, and in their consequences. Then, finally, we met with it in the effort of human nature to deliver itself from the penalty of sin. All this goes to show, that man, as a social being, has the vicarious as one of the invariable modes of his being and its development. So we noticed that objections to one use of this mode lie against others. But if it be established that such a mode belongs to human nature itself, then we approach the supernatural with very different prepossessions, than if we looked at it from out a nature in which there was nothing vicarious, or only something abnormal. Nor shall we find it strange, if, in relation to the natural, whenever the supernatural should manifest itself, and whatever good it should bring to man, it would employ this vicarious mode. Indeed not to do this, would appear strange, since an immense pedagogy had led us in this way, and accustomed us to this mode. And this we shall see when we study the incarnation.

Use of the Vicarious in Nature by the Supernatural.

WE have our Lord's authority for expecting that men's views of "earthly things, will affect, very seriously, their views of heavenly things." Our impressions of the vicarious element in nature, cannot but influence our apprehension of the vicarious in the incarnation. All the contents of this glorious truth are supernatural, and we learn them from supernatural sources. God manifest in the flesh. Every conceivable idea of mediation between God and man, fulfilled in a divinely human person. God revealed in the clearest manner, and brought in wonderful nearness to the human mind, the forgiveness of sins, the transformation of character by the Holy Spirit, and thence the restoration of conscious acceptance and communion with God. The work of redemption by Jesus Christ, through which all this has been brought to pass; the life of perfect righteousness and the death of sacrifice; the conciliation of justice and mercy, in the honoring of law, and the accomplishment of compassion. These are the "heavenly things" purely, and are revealed as such. True, we find in different parts of heathenesse, a very striking longing for divine manifestations, and in their mythologies are accounts of such. But these pagan theophanies are, at the best, only instinctive efforts of human souls, which project out of their own teeming subjectivities, exaggerated repetitions of themselves. And yet, while they distinguish and exalt by contrast the incarnation of Christ, they certainly show that the idea is not strange to man. It is also true that as we look back through the course of Jewish history, in the light of Revelation, we see a system educating a people, and through them the world, into a preparation for this incarnation, so that with a fundamental apprehension of sin, and its necessities, men might be taught, by various divine manifestations, to look forward to their fitting culmination and completeness in a person who should come, Emanuel, the Messias of God. How far men were educated, so as more readily to receive the great truth, is not now the question. The system is there, supernaturally ordered, and we can see what a wonderful preparation it forms. We look at the incarnation of our blessed Lord as accomplished, the grand object of believing vision, luminous upon the dark ground of human sin. But our point of view is greatly changed from any occupied before the coming of Christ. As we reverently say, that if God existed an infinite person, it was reasonable that he should reveal himself to beings in his image—finite indeed, yet persons—so if he revealed himself, what revelation could be conceived of more reasonable than the incarnation? If God is to make himself known as fully as possible, and through a medium the most capable of ministering knowledge, surely there is nothing in the actual creation, that we are acquainted with, or can imagine, so fitting to declare God, as humanity made in the image of God. For what are the strength, and beauty, and order in material things, or what are angelic ministries, or communications in visions of the night, and what even the voice from heaven? Nay, what the inspired utterance of prophets and holy men of old, moved by the Holy Ghost, compared with a sinless human being, as the medium of divine manifestation, distinguished above all other beings in our world by its creation in the image of God. The believer in the incarnation, adores the more, because God is so near him, within the veil of his own humanity, now, indeed, perfect in moral excellence, and evidently God's fairest work. With all the awe that it becomes created beings to feel towards their Creator, so far from the incarnation being something to which human thought, in its profoundest reach, is averse, it is beyond expression welcome to such thought, when exercised under the influence of thoroughly aroused moral sensibility. The more we thus contemplate our blessed Lord, and who will say that this is not the most fitting subjective state in which to contemplate him, the more we are impressed with the incarnation as most wonderfully adapted to us. How they err who look upon it as a dogma to be treated with indifference, its apprehension beginning and ending in intellectual perception. As Christ himself teaches, and as follows from the relation of the soul to moral truth, the appreciation of Christ as God manifest in the flesh, demands that men should regard him from out states of mind, more or less morally affected. It cannot be denied, that to men conscious of moral wants, and longing for a sense of God's nearness, to men who have felt, in any degree, this nearness in Christ, there is marvellous attraction in the incarnation. To such men it has been an exceedingly precious revelation. Hence it is held so strongly. This peculiar apprehension of Christ is susceptible of indefinite increase, as we might expect, from the relation of the subjective state to the objective person. Keeping this in mind, we may well believe in the adaptation of the incarnation to our deepest spiritual needs. Intensely conscious of our own personality, we crave a sufficient person in whom to rest, and here we have infinite fullness associated with a consciousness as definite as our own. We require might and majesty, with will, to impress us, and behold all in Christ. We demand perfect goodness, hatred of evil, delight in good, benevolence, and tenderness, and sympathy, and lo! the manifested Christ presents each in completeness, and all in unity. We desire assurance of truth, and Jesus Christ impresses us with the conviction that he is truth, a reality not possible to have been imagined, or to be the result of human accretions, but " the word of God incarnate." When our profoundest wants are discovered to us, and we feel, with a moral force we cannot resist, our sin, with its guilt and foolishness—when the great need presses us, of some one who has authority to give us peace, and power to transform us morally—then the view of Christ as incarnate God, bringing with it the certainty of his salvation, and his gracious willingness to bestow it commends itself to the awakened soul with new and peculiar evidence of its truth. The wonderful correspondence between Christ and the inmost necessities of man, comes out, when in our conviction of sin, we look upon the saviour of sinners; much more does the increasingly perceived person and work of our Lord, render stronger and clearer, this sense of his truth, when the heart has finally received Christ as its saviour. Then in the light of positive christian experience, the delightful awe, the humble assurance of safety, the ennobling complacency in Christ himself, and the consciousness of his love, the incarnation of Christ, is an object of adoring and confident faith. Such is Christ to numberless believers. Now it is the great characteristic of the incarnation that it was complete, and we dwell with awe and delight on that completeness. The son of God took upon him our very nature. It was our humanity, our mind, and sensibilities, and moral sense, and in a veritable body, "bone of our bone, flesh of our flesh." In no sense was it scenic, an appearance however beautiful, however tragical. It was actually here and in our unity. It left out nothing human. But to be completely human, meant to suffer ; suffer as we do, suffer as sinners. What sinners suffer, Revelation represents as largely penalty, and we cannot help recognizing it as such. This is palpable to us. Indeed, this suffering of Christ was certain. Without it the incarnation were incomplete. Suffering penalty was in the very warp and woof of human nature, and Christ could not become incarnate without becoming subject to sufferings now inseparable from human nature. And yet he was "holy, harmless and undefiled." The sinlessness of Jesus Christ is something wonderful to contemplate. It stands out alone in human history. The humanity in us so marred, was in him absolutely without defect. It was perfect moral excellence. Our very sin prevents the full appreciation of our own nature, when we see it in unfallen purity. But the more we study this, as it appears in Jesus Christ, compared with other men, the more intently we gaze upon the holy character of the son of man, from out our moral wants, deeply felt, and with the intuitions of penitence and love, the more wonderful it will appear, and its reality more assured. And it follows from this moral completeness, and is directly asserted by our Lord, that no constraint was upon him but that of love, and his was a willing obedience. He chose, in all freedom of choice, all that was essentially human. "He was in all points like as we are, except sin."

If, as viewed from the divine side, according to scripture, there was a need that Christ suffer; seen from the human, there was also a necessity of his suffering; for we have seen that his incarnation could not be complete without his taking upon himself the penalties that were now in the very solidarity of human nature and followed its development. Now comes the great question of the meaning for us, of this incarnation into suffering. Why should the one absolutely perfect man, alone of all his race living in sinlessness, bear the same burden as sinful men do? Why should God manifest himself as " man of sorrows and acquainted with grief?" If we allow the thought that the sufferings of Jesus Christ were on his own account, or merely arbitrary, we are involved in moral confusion. For we can conceive of a perfectly sinless humanity, serving to manifest God in the flesh, resplendent with chastened glory, and radiant with happiness. Nay, some have conjectured, this might have occurred in the possible history of man, without sin. We can dwell on such an incarnation with utmost moral complacency. Yet this supposes a humanity morally different from our actual one. No guilt, no suffering. Nothing in such a conception to confound moral distinctions, or mar moral harmony. But Jesus Christ—all that we can imagine of moral perfection, the very living temple of God, subjected to what sinners are subject to; like them encompassed about with suffering, walking throughout his life in penalties as they do, numbered at last with transgressors, and in the crowning fullness of his love, wearing a diadem of guilt. To what conclusions were we left, if all this were on his own account, or inflicted arbitrarily. But we are not left to the possibility of such a thought. There is no room for doubt as to the meaning of this humiliation, and these sufferings of the sinless Christ. They are on account of those, into whose unity he came. They are vicarious, and the climax of the vicarious in our world. Christ came to save sinful men, to form a new humanity of which he should be the head, the second Adam, men forgiven and regenerate, united to him with a conscious faith, but rooted and grounded in him, as really as before they were in their old degenerate humanity, having a life "hid with him in God," and deriving hence a new moral character manifested in fruits of the spirit, holy, Christlike tempers and conduct. This was the meaning of the incarnation, as concerning man. To this end the son of God entered into our unity, identified himself with us, subjected himself to laws, which throughout, recognized sin as something to be confessed and atoned for, was baptized with the baptism whose ground idea was repentance, was made a curse under the law, and offered himself a sacrifice. All this, mean it more or less, was for others. This was our Lord's own consciousness of himself in our world. "My flesh which I give for the life of the world," is his own description of his manifestation in our nature, and shows, unmistakably, how he regarded it. With this alone, agree all the circumstances in his incarnate existence. Indeed, there is a subversion of all moral judgment, unless this subjection to suffering were for others, and chosen by him. He could not feel himself a sinful being, nor yet did he look upon himself as an unwilling victim, in an iron system of penalty. But in that love so wondrous, he chose to suffer for others. He manifested himself where only sinners, with their penalties were, and where none could be without penalties, their own, or vicarious. He took upon himself a nature, which, unavoidably, here bore with it, the consequences of moral evil. Surely, he is always represented thus. If language can express what such a being as Jesus Christ meant; if a life, luminous beyond all others, can declare its one great intention, if the over mastering conviction of those who saw him, and loved him, and devoted their lives to preach what he was, and taught, can be understood, then, the only conception of the Lord Jesus Christ, is that of being identified with sinners for their sakes, suffering in their stead, the penalty of violated law. It is true, as noticed above, men interpret differently the descriptions of the degrees, so to speak, of the vicarious in Christ's work of atonement. But the vicarious itself, cannot be denied on any scriptural ground. Thus, we have seen, that the supernatural, the incarnation, employs in its event, and for its great purpose of benevolence, one of the modes in the very structure of human nature, the vicarious. So far, then, from being originated at the coming of Christ, or at any time since human nature began to be, or lying dormant for some emergency, it was in human nature from the first and certain to appear in every direction of man's activity, necessarily used by moral good or evil, and their consequences. As moral evil actually now works vicariously, and as we cannot conceive of a change in our race, from good to evil having taken place, under other than vicarious conditions, so, now, as far as we can look into things, it is very difficult, if not impossible, to think of any mode to be employed in a change from evil to good, other than vicarious. Perhaps this view will make some objections to a vicarious Redeemer look differently, since these objections must be made to the working of the system in which we are, and to be consistent, we must find fault with the necessity in nature, of vicarious suffering, to avert a calamity or confer a benefit. The relation of the vicarious in nature to the incarnation, will appear in clearer light, if we apprehend more strongly, the conception of this world as largely educational, as designed and arranged to teach great truths and form character. Of course this is involved, to a certain extent, in the idea of probation. There is implied in "world education," a great deal of the correlation of truths. Men are evidently to be led to some conclusions, and prepared for important moral ends, in the course of this education, by analogies and types in nature. Undoubtedly, in observing and concluding, according to this conception, men are liable to false directions of thought. Still there is much to commend it. History, too, is more in harmony with worthiest views of God and man, when it is studied as embodying this design. This aspect of the world may fairly be considered the true one, when, by the light of Revelation, we see the Jews under a system eminently educational. We have already spoken of the vicarious as a natural pedagogy, corresponding, in a degree, to that supernaturally ordained for the chosen people. If now this be regarded as but part of a great system, educating men into a preparation for truth, something grandly prospective, surely the world will appear very differently to us from what it commonly does. Thus the vicarious in nature is fitted to make very apparent, the real character, extent and consequences of good and evil, of one as much as of the other, though its relation to redemption determines our present consideration of the latter. It is important to remark again, that men's views of Christ, and the benefits to be derived from him, are very much affected by their views of sin. Now it is hard to think of any mode by which sin could be more thoroughly shown to be the dreadful thing it is, than is actually shown by its working in the vicarious mode. If sin was, in every sense, an individual matter; if it did not develop itself in relative being we should know but partially its disastrous power. But now, acting, as it does, vicariously, in race, and sub-race, and family, and natural affections, and general intercourse, and this on vastest and minutest scale, sin is illustrated with a frightful copiousness and clearness. Its actual degree is before our eyes. Its capacity of becoming greater, with even more terrible results, is constantly suggested. Tried in so many relations, its essential nature comes out most variously, and shows its identity of evil. So, too, the consequences of sin are shown by the vicarious mode, as we cannot imagine any other mode to be capable of showing. Recall what has been already noticed in society, the effects of sin continually appearing in the relations of men to one another, terrible to look at in their vicarious working. Is not this an education in the fullest sense? Ought not man, by this time, to have learned to regard sin with more dread than anything else, and to have been prepared, in some measure, to apprehend a redemption corresponding to such sin, a Redeemer fully related to such a sinner? For surely, the instruction as to sin and its consequences, to be derived from this mode of human development, the view it presents of man's bondage to evil, may well awaken such a conviction of moral want, that if any one thus conscious, did not long for a saviour in the fullest sense, he would, at least, more readily perceive such a one in his true character and work, when he should come. It is not now the question, how far this effect has been produced, but certainly here is education, and the teaching is in the same direction, on the natural side, as that on the supernatural, in the revealed system, given by God to his ancient people. But as we have already seen, yet more is contained in this pedagogy of nature. So, in this connection, we notice again, that the vicarious in nature, by its employment, to a very great extent, as a mode of natural deliverances, may well lead us to look for the employment of the same mode, in any supernatural deliverance. Not that we could gain any assurance that such a deliverance would come; not that any sufficient conclusion could be formed of a person to come; not that the real substance of the redemption itself, especially on the side towards God, could be learned from what occurs here; but to see constantly in nature, all kinds of deliverances and benefits, using this vicarious mode, and that of necessity, since we cannot imagine any other mode possible, as things are—does, most certainly, point to the employment of this same mode, by a heavenly deliverance, if there is to be one—What else expect, if we expect at all!—And thus, reverently, we may say again, that as the earth mould prefigures the form of the molten mass to be poured into it, so the vicarious mode, universal and necessary in nature, when benefits are to be conferred, prefigures the mode in which our supernatural benefit shall come, if it come at all. We have seen that this vicarious element in nature, has various degrees, from slight representativeness, to substitution. Sometimes the identification goes so far, as to seem like the merging of individuality. Here is great significance. Not that we can find in nature, any thing to warrant us in affirming what degree of the vicarious would appear in the heavenly deliverance, substitution or representativeness, more or less full, but surely it tends to prepare us to accept whatever degree is present in what is supernatural. Nay, if the heavenly deliverance should be revealed as employing this vicarious mode, in its fullest meaning, if the Heavenly Deliverer should take upon him our nature exhaustively, "in all points like us," except sin, should fulfill the years of his humanity, and accomplish human redemption in the use of the completest vicarious mode, should be in very truth, what he is seen to be, in our place, a substitute, "the just for the unjust." "He who knew no sin, made sin for us," "suffering under the law," and, at last, "numbered with transgressors," if this should be so, who shall say we have not been prepared by this pedagogy of nature, at least, not to regard as strange, the employment of the utmost degree of what was an essential mode of the humanity in which our Lord was manifested, to save it. And if any profess to shrink from this completeness of the vicarious mode, as used by our Lord, let them look at the remarkable fact, that in the domain of nature, so long as there is a willing mind in any suffering for others, instead of its being repellant to us,—the greatest possible identification with others, the most entire substitution of persons, and that, too, in endurance of extremist suffering, attract our greatest admiration, nay, call out our highest moral approbation. They stand out a welcome relief from the fearful monotony of our selfishness. But what teaching by nature are these instances to prepare men for the glorious climax in our blessed Redeemer. What if men are not led by this pedagogy in nature, into a preparation for the revealed truth of Christ, nor abate their objections to vicarious suffering in his redemption? So did the Jews refuse to be led by an inspired pedagogy of vicarious rites and sacrifices, into a preparation for the Christ who should fulfill, in his own person, their typical significance. Nevertheless, there, right before men, was that revealed system, full of the vicarious element. And so, outside of this, is human nature itself, making men familiar with it as a divinely appointed mode.

If we have studied aright the bearing of the vicarious in nature, on the great truth of Revelation, we are naturally led to think that it is only reasonable to suppose there would be confirmations of the gospel, in the structure and working of the humanity which was to receive it. The origin and authority of the revealed, will never cease to be supernatural and final. The person and work of the incarnate Christ, can never be other than the "heavenly thing," only known through Revelation. But surely it cannot lessen our reverence for the supernatural, and our appreciation of its divine bestowment, to find in structure of human nature, that, which by its striking manifestation of our wants, points to something out of itself as alone able to meet those wants.

Could we only see human nature thoroughly, we are confident that its actual state, by its correspondence to Jesus Christ as its Saviour, would be a mighty argument for "the truth as it is in him." It may be that we are far from being ready for such perceptions. We know not how much depends on the moral state, and human subjectivity must be largely taken into account. But it may be that sometime hence, when man shall look through a medium of more perspicacious humility, and observe with a profounder consciousness of need, and conclude with the estimate of more intense love, they will see more of this great harmony.

Christ Viewed in the Light of Vicarious Love.

OUR Lord once said "He who doeth his will shall know the doctrine if it be of God." Here is largely the philosophy of human belief. The perception of moral truth depends on the moral state. Revelation regards this relation of paramount importance, and the history of human opinions fully illustrates the connection. Were this clearly apprehended, it would seriously affect the way in which men approach questions to be determined. But it must be evident that men act with very little recognition of such dependence. Indeed, with many their pride of intellect would be offended at the intimation that they could not exercise it independently of their moral state. They would insist on their sufficiency to perceive any truth, irrespective of moral conditions. Of course it will be admitted, that men's opinions are more or less affected by their prejudices, but though this logically involves what we are contending for, it will be only in a most general way, and very slightly applied in what concerns the christian revelation. Here, it is safe to affirm, that men proceed to a great extent without any misgiving as to their moral condition affecting their views of Christ. The proposition that sin in a man, and his sense of it, have a great deal to do with what he will see and think of Christ, would not be generally received. Indeed, this failure of men to recognize the influence of moral evil on the mind, is not confined to religious questions. One might expect that so tremendous a fact as sin in the very self—would have great prominence given to it in any scheme of human nature, and that it would be considered carefully in relation to its disturbing force. But there is very little account made of it in the systems of philosophy. So, in a great part of human affairs, men seem to ignore it, and to have the same confidence in their conclusions, as if they were not sinners. It is then only the climax of this conduct, when they do not regard it at all important what their moral state is, in deciding upon christianity. The sensualist, the ambitious, the avaricious, the self-willed, the self-conceited, can have as true an apprehension of Jesus Christ, as the pure, the benevolent, the contrite, the humble-minded. Though the conscience may have sunk in a man to extremist moral insensibility, through brutal indulgence, or exaggerated estheticism, or any engrossing intellectual culture, until he has almost no consciousness of sin, and none of moral want, but is wholly without moral appreciation, or desire for anything else than selfish gratification—yet this man can come to the consideration of Christ, as well fitted to perceive the real person and work of the Lord Jesus, in their peculiar relation to the sinful human soul, and their desirableness as such, as though his conscience was in the highest degree, powerful and discriminating, and he had the clearest consciousness of sin, and felt deeply his moral wants. This is stated strongly, but that many maintain that the intellect is independent of moral conditions, and act accordingly, cannot be denied. Now it is in direct and profound opposition to this view and practice of men, that our Lord uttered the remarkable saying cited above. But this is the most comprehensive form ; he teaches the same in others of his discourses. Thus, in the Sermon on the Mount he says, "Blessed are the pure in heart, for they shall see God." This affirms the intimate connection between the moral state and the knowledge of God. Here is implied that an impure heart will disable a man from clearly knowing the holy God. On another occasion he says, "How can ye believe who receive honor one of another, and seek not the honor which cometh from God." (John v: 44.) This was addressed particularly to a class of men in our Lord's day, remarkable for seeking the reputation of sanctity. Those under the control of such a disposition, could not judge fairly a being like Christ. They could not see him as he really was. This was the negative side: the positive is presented when it is clearly implied that seeking honor from God, could alone have prepared these men to apprehend Christ. Here, then, we have our Lord's estimate of the connection between an inward moral state, and the perception of an object presented to the mind. It was not that these Jews knew our Lord to be the Christ, and so wilfully rejected him, but their moral state was such as to hinder them from knowing him. It was a medium through which the real person was not seen. Christ was transformed to them, and by themselves Our Lord's prayer on the cross, "Father forgive them they know not what they do," implies in the strongest manner his sense of the influence exerted on the mental vision of men, by their moral disposition. In all his intercourse it is evident that he regarded this as determining the question of faith in himself. Indeed, his own beautiful and comprehensive declaration of the necessity of a child-like spirit, is a summing up of his teaching on this point. The apostolic writings assert and take for granted the same thing. What stronger statement of the influence of the moral state upon the action of the intellect can be uttered than Paul's description of the pagan's loss of the true idea of God. Here, plainly the moral deterioration goes before the degrading conceptions of the mind. Again, what is the "veil over the Jewish mind," but the effect of a moral state, described in that most inclusive term, "Hardness of heart." So, when we read of the cross of Christ being "foolishness to the Greek," we cannot help thinking, how naturally this followed from the enormous self-conceit in the Grecian character. Paul's own history is very striking in this respect. The same person was before him at different periods, but how differently he appeared to the bigot Jew in Jerusalem, and Paul, the apostle. Probably in none of the countless millions converted to Christ, has there been a more striking illustration of the connection we are considering. In the old Testament we meet the same, strongly asserted in passages like this, "The fear of the Lord is the beginning of wisdom," and there is startling significance in the words, "The fool hath said in his heart, there is no God." But it is not in Revelation only that this power of the moral over the intellectual is asserted. In one of the apocryphal books we read, "Froward thoughts separate from God, and wisdom enters not into a malicious soul." There is a recognition of the same in pagan writers. Here is a remarkable statement of it from Seneca, "The mind that is impure is not capable of God." And yet this is only one instance; classic literature would furnish illustrations from its philosophers and tragic poets fully sufficient to show that thoughtful men in those times acknowledged this dependence, more or less, of the mind upon the heart. Of course we should expect to find this view taken among the earliest christian fathers, alike from their nearness to the primitive teaching of christianity and the observation forced upon them of the terrible effect of heathen immorality in determining men's minds. So christian writers, in all time, have insisted upon this point. Even those possessed of highest intellect themselves, and who, if any, might be supposed capable of entire intellectual independence, have expressed in clearest terms their conviction of the intellect's dependence for its conclusions upon the moral state. Thus Pascal, "Nous connaissons la verité non seulement par la raison mais encore par le cœur." It might, indeed, be expected of Pascal that he would coincide with the scripture view of the influence of character on opinions. Nor are we surprised to find this seen and noticed by one who, with marvellous intuitiveness, looked so deeply into human nature, and who may have drank at other springs, than his critics in their worship of genius, dream of,

"But when we in our viciousness grow hard,
(O, misery on't) the wise gods seel our eyes;
In our own filth drop our clear judgments; make us
Adore our errors; laugh at us, while we strut
To our confusion."

What is yet more striking, men who would shrink from finding, in this influence of the heart, any explanation of their own unbelief, do yet fully admit such influence. Thus Voltaire said of Rousseau, "His opinion was reached not through his reason, but his sentiments." What then of Voltaire, himself? His moral state was a very decided one. Did it have no influence on his opinions? There is a writer of great renown in letters. With his admirers, the impression of his genius is so great, that under its spell, they seek to excuse his sins by raising him above the moral obligations which bind common men. His superb endowments did not include a high moral sense. He was an impure man, and it did not disturb his self-complacency. He took no part in his country's struggle for life, and it did not stir the repose of his self-love. Throughout his writings, we meet the highest exercise of intellect, but are so conscious of the supremacy of the esthetical, that it is no wonder men have spoken of him as one of the great pagans, reappearing in christian times. And yet he said, "As are the inclinations so are the opinions." May not this apply, too, in his case, and be some explanation why he did not see the true Christ, to desire him. Here is another instance. It is that of one who ranked high in his day as a philosopher. He was, in some respects, far nobler than the poet just cited, but he was intoxicated with the contemplation of the ego. And he says, "Unser Denk-system ist sehr oft nur die Geschichte unseres Hertzens." I give but one more testimony from men who had not christianity in mind when they wrote. In this instance, the writer is a very acute Frenchman who has drawn one of the most frightful pictures of French democracy, and who writes of men as he does of arts and letters, with marvellous self-complacency. He is thinking of others in relation to "earthly things," but we will think of him in relation to "heavenly," when he says, "Si le cœur est parfois la dupe de l'esprit, l'esprit bien plus souvent est la dupe du cœur." Many more such admissions of the dependence of human beliefs on the moral condition, might be given. Already it may have proved wearisome to dwell so long on these admissions, but the thing itself, if true, is of such immense importance, in considering man's relation to Revelation, that we need to have it fully estab lished and made prominent; particularly as men are averse to its application to themselves. Thus, then, we have seen it quite confirmed by men themselves, that notwithstanding what is claimed for pure intellect, human opinions and beliefs, though accredited to it, are really, to a great extent, determined by the moral disposition. Indeed, with singular inconsistency, some who even resent the implication of such influence on their own judgment, do not trust that of others in matters of importance, where any strong passion is concerned. In matters of critical opinion, where one might suppose the intellect would act free from all moral bias, if this were possible; we meet with humiliating frequency, instances of fine minds so influenced by moral attractions and repulsions that our respect for their criticisms is painfully qualified. Indeed, a volume might be written on the power of mere disgusts to determine human opinions. All this should prepare us for like action in the great questions of Revelation. Here are objects the most fitted of all, to excite moral complacency or aversion, as the history of christianity abundantly shows. Then it is not likely that an exception will be found here, to man's usual way of considering objects. On the contrary, we would naturally expect the most marked exhibition of this influence of the moral state. For we must keep in mind, that if the moral be at all, it must be the most important and characteristic element of the personal self. The will, in its largest sense, is then concerned morally, so that the intellect cannot act in perception as a perfectly clear mirror, but must take into its reflections the hues of a determining self, and see objects in their light. Surely we may then affirm it to be most probable, that how the Lord Jesus Christ will appear to men, depends largely on their own moral state. Certainly he concentrates in himself, more than any object in our sphere of perception—what most concerns us as moral beings. Conceive our Lord as he declares himself to be, and as he stands forth in the world's history; a Saviour from sin and guilt. Here is the grandest object conceivable before the human mind, and yet is it in the highest degree relative, and hence demanding correspondence on the part of him who contemplates it. For it assumes that man needs such a Saviour. But he must feel that need, before he can, with the intelligence of heartfelt appreciation, behold such a saviour as Christ really is. When our Lord said "I came to call not the righteous, but sinners to repentance," it was on an occasion of a display of profound insensibility towards himself, by men who were observing and wondering at his intercourse with those upon whom they themselves looked with contempt. He was exercising his characteristic benevolence. He was manifesting his sympathy. It was not that the pure Saviour looked with moral indifference on sinners, but he beheld with tenderest interest, and attracted to him, those who felt themselves sinners. To a redeemer from sin, there could be then, as now, but two classes of men. All indeed sinners, but some felt themselves to be such, and that they needed forgiveness and moral change. However vague, this disposition put them into a relation of dependence and earnest seeking for help out of themselves, and they were prepared, in a measure, to see the Saviour in his true character. Others did not feel that they were sinners, or that they needed forgiveness and moral change, but were profoundly satisfied with themselves. There can be no doubt of the great self-conceit of some of those with whom our Lord came in contact.

It is of them he speaks with more than an approach to irony, as "the righteous." Such men plainly saw "nothing in Christ that they should desire him," but much to offend them. They beheld in him not what proved him to be the person he professed to be, but to them, in their actual moral state, he seemed to be quite another. Now this is history. Our Lord himself, judged these men as not only being without true knowledge and appreciation of him, but as unable to see him in his reality, so long as they continued in the moral state in which they were. He assumes and proceeds upon the ground, that for men to see and apprehend him aright, they must, in some measure, see and apprehend themselves aright. Nor will this appear strange, but rather to be expected, if we bring out in full relief, the person to be judged, and the persons judging. He coming to meet the deepest wants of the human soul, and those too, wholly moral. Then so far from offering any satisfaction to the ruling desires of actual men, he declared what was most opposed to those desires, establishing a kingdom within men, simply of righteousness, with very little outward inducement for men with such desires, and unlike every earthly kingdom. Now, think of those to whom the Lord Jesus Christ presented himself, and the kingdom which he sought to establish. Unconscious of the moral wants to which he was essentially related, completely mastered by wants with which he had no sympathy, passionately longing for a kingdom like those already existing, which should gratify their lust for power and riches, their hate of the oppressor, and dream of conquest over the foreigner. How could such men understand Jesus Christ? Least of all see him as their Saviour, and accept him in his true character. And why stop with the men of that age?

Why should not the view of Christ, in our day, as to what he professes to be, and do, depend largely on the moral state of men, and be affected by their dispositions? Human nature remains the same, and the relation of the subjective to the objective. Jesus Christ stands before the human mind the same. He comes not to "the righteous," not to sinners so blinded by sin as not to see themselves sinners, but with unconscious irony deem themselves righteous, who not only feel no need of being forgiven and changed in their most inward moral state, but are satisfied with themselves, and have no wants beyond those of the passing hour. How is it then possible for them to see him as he is, and to judge his truth, if by any means they have lost, or have never had, any belief in him. Nor is it necessary to delay on rejectors of Christ who are embruted by animal excess. Here a moral incapacity to appreciate Jesus Christ must be evident. But we shrink from applying the same test to men of fair exterior, and tastes opposed to all grossness, who equally reject Christ. Yet why should we? The destitution of moral correspondence and conditioning, may be as great, nay, greater, in those raised above animalism. This is easily conceivable in men controlled by one or more of the master passions, greed for wealth, ambition, or love of pleasure. Then consider the instance of those completely possessed by esthetical tastes, as for example, such as we meet in the history of that remarkable time, the renaissance, particularly in Italy. Finally subject to resolute analysis, the highest of all the rejectors of Christ, men who have devoted themselves to purely intellectual pursuits, entirely apart from moral questions, of which they come to have no recognition. Now, if in all these varieties, there is absent a sense of sin and consciousness of moral need, while on the contrary there is a settled moral insensibility, a supreme confidence in self and satisfaction with it, together with an intense desire for objects other than moral, we are warranted by the history of opinions and the nature of the relation between the subjective and objective, to find that Jesus Christ will not appear to these men what he is. They look at him from a self so unrelated to him by conscious moral need, as to be opposed to him; and hence they judge him in comparisons which transform him. We generalize about the age in relation to Christ, when he was manifested on earth. So may we now affirm of our time, that there is much in its spirit to account for its disbelief in Christ. The extent to which sin is ignored, the materialized conception of life, the immense self-conceit of men, are enough to constitute subjective states, which obscure and disfigure Christ as an object before the mind. This discussion were incomplete, without adding, that of course, the same dependence of intellect upon heart must continue in the history of believers in Christ, and condition their progress in christian knowledge. The sum of this on the negative side is; that unlikeness to Jesus Christ indisposes men to see him in his real, full character—that self, blinded by sin to any clear perception of its own sinfulness, forms a medium in which an imperfect, untrue representation of Christ will appear. On the other and positive side, it is safe to affirm, a very different result will follow when Christ is looked upon by men in moral states, the opposite of the preceding. If their consciences are roused to act under a present and powerful impression of the law of God, with consequently a deep sense of sin, and a strong conviction of their need of forgiveness, and change of character; to such Christ will appear in a relation of essential correspondence. For they are those to whom he really comes, sinners who see that they are sinners. The very ground condition of a true perception of Christ is fulfilled. From souls painfully conscious of moral wants, they look upon a person chiefly related to those wants. Christ's claims to their belief, are judged with minds under the determining influence of hearts, humbled, dependent, and longing. All this is illustrated in the early history of our faith. The men convinced of our Lord's divine mission, were men convicted of their sins, and conscious, more or less distinctly, of wants which were met by him. Now much more will this appreciation of Christ be increased, and deeper insight into his character and work be gained, when men accept him, and are changed into his likeness. Thus, if receiving him as a redeemer who saves them by a vicarious redemption, if obeying him, and constrained by his spirit, they themselves come to live lives of vicarious benevolence, accepting fully the obligation to bear others' burdens and do them good at any sacrifice to themselves, the vicarious mode in that redemption, so far from presenting anything to object to, will appear not only conformed to divine order in nature, but humbly they will, from their own experience, slight though it be, adoringly regard with moral complacency the sacrifice of Christ. By the aspect of the image, however imperfect, which is the effect and expression of their union to Christ, instinctively they are led to the original in Christ sublimely perfect. What that vicarious love is in regenerate souls, and what sacrifices it constrains to, so far from offending any high moral sensibility, any degree of pure benevolence, or indeed any thing in them, but remaining selfishness; will commend itself to them as altogether reasonable for such regenerate souls, harmonious with right, the necessary direction of true benevolence, the noblest discipline for self and the minister of purest happiness. Then, by the very aptitude of like to apprehend like, they recognize with awe indeed, and humbling consciousness, yet with unspeakable delight and sense of divinely human fitness, the perfection and greatness of vicarious love in Christ. Are we not in the direct sequence of this thought and the consistent application of the principle, if we conceive that the utmost fullness of the vicarious element in Christ—substitution—will not present serious difficulties to those who, led by the spirit of Christ, identify themselves with others to the extent of enduring extreme calamities in their place? That which in the soul imperfectly Christlike, must yet approve itself to that soul, and be in accord with its highest idea of love, can only appear consummately excellent in that glorious Saviour who manifested it in the perfection and majesty of his Divine Humanity. Doubtless the representation of Christ's vicarious suffering is sometimes so made as to give false and painful impressions, but viewed in its scriptural representation, even the fullest possible conception of Christs' identifying himself with sinners, we believe will depend greatly upon men's own type of christian life, or at least upon their conviction of the extent to which vicarious love may go in this world. Nay, could we imagine a great perfecting of the image of Christ in christians, we should see them putting themselves in the place of others, and willingly undergoing sufferings for them, and this, not from any invented mode of exercising benevolence, but from the necessity imposed by the present order of things in our world. Did a Christlike life abound, and yield often and vicariously, reflections of him in self-sacrificing benevolence; we believe that in the light of such reflections, his very self would be illustrated and proved in the lives of those who felt and acted thus. The transcendent sacrifice of our Lord would be set forth more clearly, and its completeness rendered more evident, when it should be seen to be the glorious crown and harmony of all vicarious love on earth. Nay, it may be, that here waits a solution of our mysteries. Only a practical one, the being and doing, necessary to the knowing. But this simple yet magnificent understanding and proof of Christ is only in small part ours yet. We live on too low a moral plane. Our wretched selfishness keeps us down and makes our comparisons unworthy, and our light obscure. The medium, which our moral state makes, and in which we contemplate Christ, lessens his person and makes his work indistinct. It requires more likeness to him to see him clearly. But, if it be true that the fullest view of Jesus Christ and the strongest faith in him, are things greatly to be desired, so is it true that the way to attain this luminous view of him, this assuring confidence in him, is heartily to obey him, and to act in the spirit of his vicarious love. And this rests on his own word, setting forth a law of our being in the apprehension of truth, and we come back to his great saying. (John vii: 17.) Here, then, possibly, may some who question, find one explanation of their difficulties, and one way out of them. In our self-sufficiency we would dictate the terms of our belief. We quite ignore the influence of sin upon the action of our minds. We demand some apologetic suited to our age, some new statement and argument addressed to our present intellectual view. But the fixed conditions of attaining and keeping moral truth, cannot be set aside. We cannot change the connection between our dispositions and opinions. There is nothing in this age, nor in any age, to lessen the effect of moral states upon intellectual apprehension. This must be taken largely into account in an exhaustive view of human nature. The philosophy which makes no note of it, is defective at ground, and that notion of life, even in common affairs, which leaves it out, will prove superficial and partial.

It must occur to any one who studies earnestly the great questions of life, that it is very important to have adequate ideas of moral evil, and a sufficient sensibility to it. This is true in every part of human development. But we have seen that it is of vital moment in the matter of human redemption. Now it can hardly be doubted that inadequate views of sin prevail among men. Indeed this is to be expected. It is altogether probable that the evil and extent of sin would be lessened in human apprehension of it, since everyone would unconsciously seek to have as little self-condemnation as possible. Difference of views here, must have something to do with difference of views of other truths intimately related. How can it be otherwise, than that the Redeemer from sin should fail of highest appreciation in the minds of men whose apprehension of sin is comparatively slight. We should not have such mixed notions of christianity itself—the moral substance, the fruit of the spirit, so wanting, and instead so much mere sentiment and devout estheticism, except the moral sense were only partially alive to sin. We cannot safely neglect the order of truth which our Lord taught. So fearful a thing as moral evil in human nature, must have all the weight it demands. Any system constructed, any seeming progress in the individual or society, without due heed to this, will sooner or later betray its unsoundness. A true intelligence of sin, increasing in thoroughness and fineness of moral sensibility, will be found essential to a true aspect of life—a sound philosophy—a correct interpretation of history—a symmetry of doctrine—a just apprehension of Christ and growth in christian character.

Christian Morality Vicarious.

MORALITY must be the same essentially, always and everywhere. If not, then any conception of right contradicts itself. Sometimes, indeed, it is practically difficult to keep hold of this identity in different circumstances, but the very idea of morality demands that it be apprehended as something unchangeable in human affairs. Brought into consciousness through the action of relative being, and manifested in obedience or disobedience to law, it is yet necessarily conceived of, not as created by relations, but antecedent and superior to them. Hence, it is the same in relation to God, or self, or fellow beings. Hence, too, there can be but one morality for all civilizations and classes of men. Hence, again, the morality of regenerate men must be that of men born and continuing holy. Indeed, regeneration is represented in scriptures as a return. The mode in which morality will manifest itself may vary, but the spirit never. Of course, christian morality will be just the opposite of immorality existing among men. So it will be conditioned in like manner by the structure of society—as immorality is. We have seen that human selfishness is determined as to its form, largely by the vicarious element in nature, necessitating a mode of being and development, which has nothing to do with character itself, but a great deal with the way in which character manifests itself. The more closely we looked into human nature, the more pervading we found this vicarious element. We saw that there was a vast and minute system of representativeness, substitution, and identifying of one with another, in which men were so bound together by the finest, yet indissoluble reticulations, that no one could sin in and to himself alone. The selfishness most concentrated with apparently no thought of others, had yet to carry more or less, the destiny of others, and must act in and for them, even if for their injury. This was seen to stand out with hideous distinctness in what were considered the great immoralities of men, but it was seen also in what were deemed slight transgressions. And this was observed to be constant in operation, yielding to no changes of civilization, refusing to be reasoned away, forcing itself upon the notice and convictions of men, making moral evil appear in its true, fearful aspect, on the human side. Very naturally might it be concluded, that the moral good which should take the place of this moral evil, would be a corresponding opposite, that is, unselfishness conditioned by the vicarious element. The good, like the evil, will act vicariously of necessity, since it finds this mode fixed in any development of human nature, and uses it in dispositions and deeds of love. Here, then, is a pedagogy to lead us into an acceptance of Christ's morality, which we have seen to have been in a remarkable degree vicarious. True, it would seem sufficient for a christian to know that his Lord commands him to follow in his steps. True, again, it might be thought that the contemplation of such moral excellence as Christ's, by one who believed in him, would of itself suffice to produce conformity to that excellence. But actually, this is only partially the result. Even after our Lord's wondrous love, as shown in living and dying for others, is fully admitted, and even regarded as the only ground of salvation, it is not as fully admitted that Christ's morality is proposed, as that which is to be reproduced in the lives of christians. Indeed, it is sometimes said that such a morality as Christ's could only be intended as a representation of perfect goodness, yet in no wise as a rule binding on actual men. But there is, however, no avoiding the plain sense of scripture, which expressly calls upon christians to lay down their lives for others, not indeed to make atonement, yet to act in its spirit, that is, with the vicarious benevolence of the atonement by our Lord. Then the unity of morality demands this conformity to Christ. If he lived a morally perfect human life, this is what our nature would be if fulfilling its own necessary ideal.

Hence, to live a new moral life in Christ, like his, is, after all, only a return to true morality. This were sufficient to establish the obligation upon christians to practice a morality like their Lord's, vicarious, but if we have studied nature aright, we find in its mode of development, a perpetual enforcement of the scriptural doctrine. So our way is clear to consider freely, christian morality in its vicarious aspect. Until we behold the vicarious love of Jesus Christ, we are amazed and shocked at the extent and enormity of the use made of nature's vicarious mode, by human selfishness. There is, indeed, at all times, some relief to this view, in hopeful, yet imperfect instances of the same mode employed by human benevolence. But in our Lord we have the significance of nature fully made known, and are shown how its very structure necessitates a mode of action, which typifies the form, which the highest possible benevolence would assume, when it should appear on earth.

The incarnation, be it reverently said, makes use of this

mode to its utmost extent. The special work of atonement employs it exhaustively to accomplish its purpose of satisfaction and propitiation. As really is the morality of our incarnate Lord set forth in this mode. If in thought we separate what really cannot be separated, our faith should preserve the unity. If Christ presents himself to be believed in, as redeeming us by a vicarious sacrifice, he does not less as an example of the vicarious love, which he will have us exercise. Does not this follow from the first: can vicarious love characterize the redemption and not the redeemed? For what did Christ redeem men, if it was not that they should become morally new creatures in him? And how could they be morally good in him, without being morally good like him? What other morality could this be than one which acted vicariously? Certainly it borders on selfish impunity, to make much of the redemption, and qualify that for which we were redeemed. Hence, christians should look to their Lord, not only as their saviour from guilt, and source of new life, but as the illustration of what that life should be: Christ's own morality, the rule of human conduct, near and definite and authoritative, and from which there is no appeal. That men should clearly understand what manner of spirit he would have them of, and what "the much fruit he would have them bear," as branches of himself, the vine. Every thing in his revelation has been ordered so as to make his life among men stand out with greatest possible distinctness. He is, unquestionably, the most commanding object for reverential admiration and moral complacency, in all history. Central to all humanity, surrounded by most various forms of selfishness, contrasted with every type of human character, discriminating with unanswerable decision, all the products of society, his grand and beautiful personality presents a uniform exercise of vicarious love. It is the same idea, the same spirit throughout. His death on the cross was the culmination of all that he endured in our nature, and differed only in degree from his other sufferings. He knew no sin, and yet we see him throughout his incarnation on earth, suffering as sinners suffer. Hence, there is no escape from moral confusion, except in the unity of his sufferings, all vicarious, all suffered for others. So his whole life was lived for them. There was absolute completeness in it. Nothing interrupts this unity of vicarious love. Every healing act which he performed, every gracious word he uttered, was identical in moral significance with what he endured. This was Christ's morality. Christians must fully apprehend this idea, if ever they are to be built up in Christlike character. They must enter into his marvellous sympathy with men. Human selfishness produces a fatal incredulity in respect to Christ's sympathy. This extraordinary characteristic of our Lord must fail to be appreciated so long as self exaggeration prevails in actual men. Nevertheless, we cannot truly understand Christ's morality without an appreciation of his sympathy. The expression "enthusiasm for human nature," has been applied to our Lord. But though significant of his wonderful devotion to the good of man, this does not exhaustively describe his identifying himself, with others, throughout the whole of his life. It is this which lies at the ground of all his conduct. It is this, which the wretched felt in his presence, and which drew them to him. This, too, though they could not for a moment think he was indifferent to their sins, since our Lord's unfailing discrimination of moral evil, and abhorrence of it, appear in the clearest light, and are the essential manifestations of his sinless purity.

It is, indeed, strange to us, that with such feelings he could, at the same time, manifest such tenderness towards even the vile. Equally strange that they, who must have felt their own sin made more repulsive by contrast with his purity, were yet so attracted to him, so confident of his receiving them. But so it was. And this continues to be not the least wonderful thing in that life. True, we may, with reverence, find in the analysis of Christ's sympathy, a remarkable element, the sense of man's worth in being. This is very apparent in his whole course on earth. Indeed, it follows from his incarnation. To him who came to save men, all were sinners, but all were moral beings in God's image. We do not suppose that any definite idea of this was in the minds of those whom our Lord thus received, though it is natural to think they must have been elevated to some self-respect by the loving benefits of such a being. But it is enough here, to state strongly that which by itself is most striking. The men apparently farthest removed from human fellowship, came to Jesus Christ assured of his sympathy. And this must have had great power over those who met it. For we must remember that the kindlier times in which we live, can give us but faint conceptions of the absence of sympathy in that age. The separations between classes of men, were absolute chasms. We do not appreciate what christianity has already done in bringing men nearer to each other. Yet, even now, the utmost sympathy that the least selfish show, only exalts by contrasts that of Christ's. The more we study this, the more its remarkable character impresses us, and the conviction gains upon us, that only such sympathy is adequate to the wants of human society. Now, it is this sympathy of benevolence, which must characterize christian morality. Only thus can men be truly Christlike. Anything else is nothing but unchanged nature at ground. So far, then, as men are changed into the likeness of Christ, they will love as he loved. Like him, they will love their fellow-men; independently of condition or conduct, and this, when like their Lord, they morally disapprove. So this love will persevere against all oppositions. Hence, it freely accepts the vicarious mode in its ministrations of good to others, as Christ did, and manifests itself in this way. As constantly seen, there is no originating this way, not even by Christlike love itself. No choice is involved in determining such a way to be, but choice is exercised in determining to use a way already established, a willing identification of self with others. Here, of course, nothing approaches the idea of atonement, but here will be the spirit of him who alone could, and did make atonement. Necessarily, then, such love, in its natural course, will meet and endure sufferings peculiarly belonging to others. To follow out into our actual life, such a morality would be difficult, and yet, what there is of Christlike morality on earth, is nothing different in kind from this very vicarious love. But it is capable of being so much greater in degree, and there is, so to speak, so much more capacity in the vicarious mode to be made use of, that we can form very inadequate conceptions of what would follow the utmost increase and extent of vicarious love. Try, now, to imagine Christlike sympathy working out its necessary significance in the actual world. The legitimate action of such morality must change men's views to an extent beyond our power to estimate. Men could not accept Christ's type of human character, and shape theirs accordingly, without an exceeding great transformation of ideas and feelings as regards certain qualities, in relation to others. Thus, humility and meekness, exercised in all the intercourse of life as christian morality demands, could only become habitual when that most comprehensive and insidious characteristic, self-conceit, together with resentment, so ready to be excited and so slow to abate, should be regarded with a moral abhorrence which we never dream of feeling. In a word, the central force of christian morality, disinterested benevolence, cannot be heartily received without our giving up many of the notions of self-indulgence which now we defend. Then, too, the end of living which christian morality proposes, the building up of Christ's kingdom in this world, can only be followed at the expense of the ends which commonly engross us. Of course it is not easy to determine how far these ends could be pursued, were christian morality paramount, but it is certain, that if christians were intent on promoting the object Christ had in view, and which he commanded them to keep in view, they could not devote themselves as they do to these things, nor could they agree as they do, with the world's estimate of them. Nor, if christian morality is to rule absolutely in our minds, could education, in its largest sense, remain what it is. But if the object of all cultivation is to furnish men more abundantly with power to carry out the purposes of a Christlike spirit, then there must be a very great change in our training, and many of our ideas must give place to others, more in harmony with the christian idea. These considerations of what is involved in the full significance of christian morality, prepares us to expect the greatest possible difference in the conception of personal sacrifices, which must go with such a morality. We have seen that since sin has enrooted itself in human nature, and makes use of the vicarious mode in its manifestations, this has become, in no slight degree, its entrenchment against the aggressions of benevolence. For now, when good to others is contemplated, this vicarious structure presents itself threateningly to our selfishness, and insists on the fulfillment of its condition. It demands an identifying of self with others, which involves, to greater or less extent, the endurance of what peculiarly belongs to them. Christian morality surveys the evils of sin, the woes, the antagonisms, and various complications of society. It beholds the dreadful mass of heathenesse, and hears, too, Christ's great command. But even our Lord bids men count the cost of being his disciples, and doing his work in such a world. Human nature itself, from its inmost structure, reechoes and emphasizes the words of Christ. "You may, indeed, reform some evils, and accomplish some good for man, at little sacrifice, but you cannot with partial and holiday benevolence, reach my deeper and greater hurts. If you attempt the Christlike work in its fullest meaning, if you mean radical reform in society, if you really intend to obey Christ and do what his spirit unmistakably enjoins, and set about in earnest, the great and immediate object before christians, the conversion of the nations, then must you accept a vicarious life, far beyond any conception you now have. You must put yourselves in place of others and act for them, with a degree of identification that will necessitate extremist sacrifices." Thus waits for us the fixed condition of Christlike beneficence. Again, notice that here is no self-origuated endurance of penalty, no work of supererogation, but a necessary mode of our nature, and there is no avoiding or changing it. Indeed, the greater the work of benevolence to be accomplished, the greater will be the degree in which the vicarious mode must be used. Perhaps it is well for men that they have very imperfect conceptions of what they undertake, or they would never undertake any important enterprise for good. But God always means more than man, and so it is found that doing good, like being good, is not in separate actions, complete each in itself and independent of others. On the contrary, there is an essential connection and conditioning. One work leads to another, or rather cannot be done thoroughly, without doing another, and yet another, and so onward indifinitely, till the real work discovers a vastness and a unity, never thought of in the beginning. Then, with this increasing greatness of the work, comes out the necessity of greater sacrifices. Thus God leads men into conceptions and practice of a wider benevolence. Thus he teaches vicarious love, of the very highest degree, by the working of human nature in the manifestation of its wants. It must be evident, that were a Christlike morality recognized in the fullest sense, there must follow a very different relation to the world on the part of christians from what exists now. No such admission of what are termed the claims of society could be possible, nor such conventional morals as christians actually allow. On the contrary, there must come into the christian consciousness, along with the vicarious love to be exercised as Christ exercised it, the view of the world which

Christ had and taught his disciples to have. Indeed, the world's need of such love supposes the world's moral condition to be radically bad, and so, largely false to its true idea. The Being who loved it so that he "gave his life" for it, who knew the world as none other knew it, has put this beyond the power of mistake by those who accept his judgment of man. For he has testified in the strongest manner, that the world was fundamentally antagonist to his gospel, and would oppose to the last the building up of a new humanity in his image. Thus he carefully prepared his disciples for what they had always expected to meet. And they plainly show that they understood him to mean nothing less. We have most striking proof of this in the epistle of the beloved disciple, probably the very latest written, where we have very prominent, the statement of a profound opposition between the spirit of the world and the spirit of Christ. They who would do such a world the greatest good, could only do this when acting in full apprehension of the world's moral state, as their Lord regarded it. Then, indeed, a Christlike morality would have to meet constant occasions of vicarious benevolence. And, now, unless the world is changed at ground, and the real spirit of human society is entirely different, so that our Lord's words no longer apply, the relation of the world to christianity is the same as ever. Indeed, it seems to be the opinion of many, that such a change has taken place, and that our Lord could not say now what he said of the world in his day, and if John were to write now of the moral situation, he could not describe the world in such antagonism to the kingdom of Christ as he did in his epistle. Of course, all must see a great change in the outward aspect of society. We cannot say how much modern civilization, considered apart from other influences, has done to affect the world's conduct to christianity, since it was in ancient civilization the gospel appeared, and it was then that the world was so opposed to it, and since, too, this modern civilization may owe far more of itself to this very christianity, then we can estimate. But it cannot be denied that the gospel itself has exerted an immense influence on mankind, and changed to considerable extent, the appearance of society. We see nothing like the open and violent opposition of ancient times. On the contrary, there is large public recognition of christianity. The heavenly leaven is working with undiminished force in humanity. Its quickening energy is seen in regenerate lives, and perhaps not less apparent is its indirect action in restraining, elevating and refining men. But this is very far from proving that Christ's kingdom and the world have become identical, or that human society, at heart, is other than antagonistic to the gospel of Christ. The opposition of positive unbelief, the utter indifference to christianity, the self-indulgence independent of restraint, and this on the largest and smallest scale, prove the contrary. Above all, the aversion of the church at large, to accept the most unworldly conception of christian faith, the most spiritual idea of christian life, and the highest standard of christian morality, should be sufficient to convince any observer that the relation between the world and a living christianity, is unchanged. It is then in full view of this, that they must act, who would follow Christ in his morality, and they can only do this on the condition we have been studying, of vicarious endurance. Now it is just this from which men have shrunk. Hence they have sought to accommodate christianity to their own state. One can see in all the ages since the coming of Christ, the constant working of this tendency. History is full of the attempts of men to adjust christianity to the condition of society they wished to maintain, and, in particular, to qualify the morality which Christ demands, so as not to interfere with their own standard of right. Men will not accept a Christlike morality as the measure of their conduct, if they can possibly satisfy their conscience with anything less, called by the christian name. One of the religious phenomena in our day, is the almost instinctive effort to secure religious surroundings, in harmony with changed social tastes and interests. But whatever we do to evade the fullest significance of a Christlike morality, we cannot alter its nature, nor do away with our obligation to practice it. The moral state of humanity is the same; its vicarious mode of development remains the same. The Lord Jesus Christ in his person and work, so also in his morality, cannot change, without denying himself, so that they who live in him a new life, must, like him, live a life of vicarious love. Then any great advance of christianity must be an advance in Christlike morality. Any attainments in higher life, to mean much, must mean attainments in substantial goodness of character, which, in relation to fellow beings, will manifest itself vicariously to the utmost. But if this conclusion be reached, then it may be said: "To carry out christianity in this understanding of it, is an impossibility." That is only saying christianity is an impossibility. But there is no other understanding of christianity, if we accept the obligation to be Christlike, as determining the type and measure of christian morality. A qualified christianity such as men might be willing to receive, such in fact as they are always trying, can never fulfill the authoritative revelation of Christ and his kingdom, can never answer to what in kind and degree, human nature, by its very structure and mode of development, imperatively demands. A christianity which men would be willing to accept as agreeing with the actual state of their intellectual judgments and moral habitudes, would always be changing. Such a christianity could not command human respect in its repeated changes and varying apologies, while the exigencies of human society, ever discovering themselves deeper and wider, point to nothing less than the utmost exercise of vicarious love. The world waits for the completest application of the spirit of redemption by regenerate men, to its complicated evils. It is the place for the manifestation of Christlike benevolence. Only identification with others, beyond any present conception, can overcome the fastnesses of human selfishness, or solve the problems of human sin. We believe this will one day be apparent, though ages may have to pass, before the failure of all else shall have taught men that a Christlike morality alone is suited to earth

Thus have we seen that human nature itself, by its very structure and mode of development, is in no slight sense "a schoolmaster to lead men to Christ," and after, to teach them how to manifest the life which he imparts to them.

Even if we do not accept the whole argument, surely it is well to try to live the life of vicarious love, for this is the mind of Christ, and the great need of human society.

SERMONS.

The Ethical Side of Human Nature, a Great Concern of the Preacher.

(*Delivered before the Missionary Society, Brown University, June 17, 1877.*)

THE preacher is not made any more than the poet. What is not in a man, cannot be brought out. Yet education may do much, and those whom I address feel, perhaps, as a certain speaker felt at the beginning of his course, and with more humility and higher purpose, say as he said, "It is in me and shall come out." Surely our country needs good preachers. For it is no light matter to preach in our day, when society has grown to be such an immense power and this collective humanity contains so much. Naturalism, too, has become so encroaching, that Lucretius himself would be pleased, and the higher paganism feel at home in some departments of modern thought. Evidently there is a great necessity of due preparation for the work of the ministry. Departing somewhat from the usual course on this occasion, let us consider "The ethical side of human nature, as concerned in the work of the preacher." For human nature may be said to have its sides—in that it has various susceptibilities ; and it is the confusion of these and their disproportionate culture, to which we owe much of our poor results. Thus christianity does indeed address the intellect. Of course, this must present the objects of faith, and enter into all christian experience. But intellect ever so strong, or fine, or luminous, is not even in its highest exercise, nor its greatest achievements, the chief part of man. It is not the end but only a means of his development. It is not character, nor capable of possessing character, though greatly affected by character. It ministers with equal ease to good and evil. A highly intellectual man may be indifferent to moral distinctions, and have moral perceptions very feeble in proportion to the apprehensions of his intellect. The æsthetical belongs in part, to the intellect, though chiefly to be distinguished as sensibility. Christianity addresses this too. How much, is a question. Certainly our faith does not demand the ugly, nor is holiness promoted by bad taste. Nay, ugliness and vulgarity may be injurious to sound morals. Christianity may use to advantage architecture, and music, and rhetoric. The æsthetical has apparently a natural affinity with the merely religious sensibilities, may excite them to a high degree, but it has no essential connection with the moral nature in man. On the contrary, esthetical culture may proceed without any regard to the moral, and even crowd it out. The ancient Greek civilization abounds in proof of this. So does the Italian Renaissance. A great deal in our own civilization, which may almost be termed the modern pagan school, illustrates this. No slight amount of our literature is thus characterized. Ritual churchdom, during the past centuries, puts beyond question, the influence of the æsthetical over the moral. Our own time witnesses an increasing attention to art, in worship by churches which once thought little of this as accessory. One, indeed, might question even on the ground of taste, whether much of the art employed, be not offensively florid, and whether the professed symbolizing of noble ideas does not render empty or false conceptions instead. But the graver matter remains. What of the relation of all this to the moral? Man is never wholly independent of his surroundings, and it is very doubtful whether, in some of our churches, the artistic be not gaining over the moral, and the question of christians going to the theatre, be not settled by the theatre coming to the church. Very curious it will be for those, in coming years, to watch the course of some of the descendants of the Puritans, who have lately emigrated into buildings the most remote possible from the simplicity of their fathers, lavish in elaborate ornamentation and various coloring, full of multiform carvings and dim "religious light," though more "dim" than "religious," with music skillfully manipulated to utter all conceivable sounds; from screams of anguish to notes of Bacchanals, with fantastic pillars and awe inspiring corners: the whole so very "churchy" that instinctively one snuffs incense and looks about for confessional boxes with their hidden ears for whispered sins. One is rather disappointed, in seeking the unity of the thing, not to see a procession of robed priests and small boys in white night gowns issuing from some scenic door. Will the moral keep its supremacy over the beautiful, if this be the beautiful? Will the sermon maintain its place, and the primitive meeting for prayer live a vigorous life in such surroundings? The relation of christianity to man's religious nature, is of course more intimate. Here is greater need of cautious analysis because "religious" is used to mean more or less. But it is certain that much of man's religiousness is purely natural, and has no more moral quality than other sensibilities, without character. Thus writers on morals, like Lecky, remark the singular independence of moral conduct which characterized the pagan religiousness. But we have most to do with religious phenomena in christendom. Unless we believe in an impossible number of wilful deceivers, we must suppose many men have been religious without much or any moral excellence. There are times in history, when, what largely passes for christianity, seems so changed, that we can hardly find any of the moral characteristics which Christ declared essential, to the kingdom of righteousness established by him. Men were devotional, sometimes passionately so, and yet full of wickedness, in many instances, without misgiving. It was the old pagan separation between religiousness and morality, reappearing. Such monsters as those of whom that monarch of Spain, on whose delineation the historian dwells, as if held by a hideous fascination, is an illustration. Rochefoucauld describes as a common occurrence, in his day, the "galante" turned "devote." What regeneration as taught by Christ, was there in all this? What is much of later antinomianism, but high religiousness in alliance with mere intellectualism. It is not uncommon now, to meet instances of fervidly religious spirits, empty of moral substance, emotional in prayer, easy weepers, irrepressible singers—Oh, how some people do sing!—but bad livers. It is impossible to account for phenomena in the religious world if we do not keep in mind this distinction. Any degree of religious sensibility, without wholesome sense of sin, seems possible to this strange heart of man. Men sometimes take pleasure in being religiously affected, while they shrink from moral discrimination. Under some circumstances it is dangerous to rely upon this side of human nature, or to address it so largely, as is frequently done, since the fruits of the Spirit, regenerate character, though manifested in it, are not originated there. Only as determined and permeated by the moral, is the religious nature rightly exercised. These modes of our being may thus be cultivated out of proportion, and reliance placed upon them, for results of which they are incapable. In consequence certain specious appearances regarded as christian, may have a pious lacquer and savor about them, but sufficient tests prove them only phenomenal christianity. Will not an undue prominence given to one or more of these elements, account for some of the unsatisfactory phases of our religion? For the moral in man is of the greatest moment, and constitutes his true character. Here is the chief substance of his personality. His will, in its highest exercise, manifests itself in moral determination. The inner man— The I—The fontal self—is moral. It is this which relates man to the divine law, so that consciously or unconsciously, in immanent state, or recognized act, he is right or wrong, holy or sinful. His relations to God and other personal beings, are chiefly distinguished by this. In all that he is or acts intellectually, esthetically, religiously, or in any way with purpose, he is characterized according to what he is morally. This makes him the fitting subject of divine government in its fullest significance, to whom belongs retributive distinctions, the capacity for probation and redemption. So is it this moral nature, which puts him in wonderful accord or discord with physical nature. More remarkably still, it determines his development in the vicarious structure of society, so that history is unintelligible if the moral be not largely taken into account. Sin and guilt reside in this. Here are man's deepest wants, forgiveness of sin, and transformation of character. Hence man's relation to Jesus Christ chiefly concerns the moral, and the human aspect of Christ's work presents, with unmistakable clearness, changes in the moral sphere. Our Lord shows this to be the matter of his own consciousness, and his teaching puts it beyond any question. His interview with Nicodemus is plainly intended to declare the nature of his kingdom, and is exhaustive in its statement of the moral ends designed. "The earthly things," so fundamental in actual human nature, and whose right apprehension is affirmed to be essential to the right apprehension of "heavenly things," are clearly distinguished as man's moral state, and so radically evil as to need a moral transformation by the spirit of God. While "the heavenly things" are as plainly distinguished in their supernatural origin, as "the Son of God manifest in the flesh," and his redemptive work, whereby man is delivered from the guilt and sinfulness of his moral state. Our Lord's sermon on the mount, is a marvellous summary of what that moral change in man is— which the Holy Spirit produces. That sermon is a description of the new humanity, the new creature in Christ, and throughout, its characteristics are intensely moral. So in the same strain writes Paul when he describes "the fruits of the Spirit," when he exhorts to seek "the mind that was in Christ," and most of all in the great thirteenth of Corinthians, where the chosen expositor of christianity has given us the divinely authorized conception of a regenerate man in forms of wondrous purity and beauty. That chapter has the substance of christian character and the very aroma of the gospel. It is the farthest removed from actual human nature, and describes what only the Holy Spirit can produce in the selfish human heart. Note here again, how eminently moral it all is. So James, evidently with the sermon on the mount in his mind, felt the necessity in his day of dwelling on this ethical side, and labors to show what must be the effects and proof of living faith. John, so intent on the inward life, and so exalting the nature of the change within man, is equally careful to insist on its being a moral revolution in all relations towards God and man. Thus everywhere in the New Testament, the new man in Christ is a morally changed being—Christlike — the likeness being a moral one. This may seem only a truism, yet since it confessedly does not stand out in our experience, as its importance demands, it may be well to enforce the view taken, by studying more particularly the morality which christianity aims to produce.

I. It regards moral excellence as in itself right, not as a means, but as an end; not as something arbitrarily appointed, but as of everlasting being, the holiness of God manifest in law. Not man first and afterwards right, but man created with a moral nature, into moral law, which awaited him; not dependent, then, on conventional agreements, but superior to human consents; a law, harmonizing in idea with utility, and happiness, and beauty, but not identical with them or even growing out of them, but rather, at times, demanding their sacrifice. In this respect right not unfrequently, sets at naught the advocacy of morality from considerations of advantage, and has no sympathy with the notion, however unctuously maintained that Godliness is profitable in all business operations. Indeed, he who would urge fishermen to keep the Lord's day, on the assurance of better fares in the week, is under a delusion if he thinks fish will not bite on Sunday. As to happiness it is a question of kinds. Evidently even immoral men, within certain limits, do enjoy themselves. The essential claim, then, of christian morality, is its being right in itself; to which we cannot oppose our profit or pleasure. This intrinsic obligation is affirmed by our intuitive apprehension, not dependent on intelligence, except for clear statement, but distinct from merely intellectual perceptions, as from sensuous impressions, and religious sensibilities. All that the highest and best conceived of, though in fragments all that is excellent in Eastern, or Grecian, or Roman ethics, is contained in christianity, while the moral law of the older revelation, cleared from glosses, is reaffirmed by Christ and declared to be identical in all time, and unchangeable as God himself.

II. Next contemplate this morality as complete in its scope. Nothing conceivable is wanting in its comprehensiveness. It pervades with its law the whole personality, conscious or unconscious, and includes all relations. Thus all virtues of man as related to God, as creature, subject and child, are most clearly set forth; the reverence, the humility, the penitence, the faith, the love, the cheerful submission, the willing obedience. What moral excellence is it possible to think of as exercised towards God, that is not strongly insisted on by christianity? So we cannot find any personal virtue in relation to self, neglected, but each one necessary to the idea of a true man, is brought into light and imperatively urged. What inwardness of righteous being! What purity! What reduction of this exaggerated—What healing of this distempered self! What different souls were ours if only we had what is luminously described, in this connection, as christian morality! If we go into the vicarious and complicated relations sustained by men to each other, where the character must manifest itself, we meet the explicit obligations of christian morality at every point. Nothing is left beyond control of law. Nothing too high or too low. No room for conventional codes. Men think to reserve to themselves irresponsible parts of life—but it is vain. The home, the State, the church, the school, the mart of business, the intercourse of society, all possible circumstances in which men have to do with men, are in the scope of this morality. It is, indeed, wondrously complete in application to human affairs. What honoring of law and government, yet what dignity of the individual person! What deference to age! What recognition of others' claims and fairness toward them! What integrity and truthfulness in all things! What considerateness toward dependents and inferiors! What heartfelt courtesy of manners! What forbearance and meekness! What kindliness! What sympathy with everything human! What large benevolence! A late distinguished writer with no intentional disparagement of christianity, rather implies that while it is preëminent in demanding the gentler virtues, yet some forms of paganism have excelled it in the heroic. But not to insist that when men feel it their duty to fight, moral force must be considered, and that in all probability Cromwell's ironsides would in nothing have proved inferior to Cæsar's tenth legion, it is sufficient to answer that the severest culture of the heroic among the Romans, could not require such abnegation of self as christian love, and that the early confessors who put right above life, may well compare with the bravest fighters of earth. The same writer, and others with him, have exalted Roman patriotism above christian love of country. But, not to delay on the Latin father's assertion of the disciples' loyalty, it would be well to subject to a moral test, the devotion of Roman citizens to their state, before we admit all that is claimed for it. In Greece, the absence of national consciousness prevented a noble state life, and in fact the Greeks had nothing but mutually destroying city existence. If in Rome there was more organic state life, yet the sentiment of class was predominant. Sober history tells a different tale from Macaulay's Lays. It begins with factions and ends with Cæsars. In relation to all other people, Rome's famous state was a banded unity to conquer, a perpetual organization to devour, all nations. "The wolves of Italy," they lived on carnage. Such embodied selfishness might teach the world great lessons of order, but what high morality can there be in patriotism like this? And, what in much that is called patriotic now, and which even christian men accept. What shall we say of Russia's patriotism in relation to other lands? What of the German's love for his fatherland, as typified by that pious bird, the Prussian eagle, looking every way at once? What does England's patriotism teach of regard for others as shown in past years, and at present illustrated by Mephistopheles, her prime minister? No, patriotism like other natural affections, is capable of fearful wrong, if not pervaded by moral principle. It may be only a form of selfishness, on a large scale, to work untold injury to the world. Patriotism, itself, must be subject to something higher. Now christianity enjoins love of Rome, but love of Christ more. It does not neglect country, as it does not home, but it is a world religion. Lecky was right— in one aspect of comparative morality, christianity does certainly exalt mankind above lesser relations, since its ground fact is, that Christ died for the world, its unmistakable commission is to preach the gospel, without delay, to all nations.

Hence, what we make a specialty of, and term "foreign missions," is simply a direct and immediate expression of christian morality. It is just the aspect in which the world appears to the benevolence supposed to be exercised by christians. Of course this is a strong way of putting it, but it is the primitive way—that acted upon by the early christians. This explains much in their conduct, and accounts for some of the objections of their enemies who could not understand this regard for all men. If this be true, we have much to unlearn. Only one church in christendom, and that the smallest, seems in modern times to have taken this view. Of course, should it be taken, some very grave consequences would follow, changing materially much that is now accepted by christians. Particularly would such a view make it easy for men to decide who should go to the heathen. Since the question, then, would rather be not "who shall go," but "who shall stay." Equally with the extent, is the spirit of this morality remarkable. It is the love with which we have been loved. Christlike, identifying self with others. Such is the completeness of christian morality. Then think of its comprehensiveness, its union of strength and tenderness, its lofty ideal of goodness, its abhorrence of evil, its complacency in law, sensibility to right, its inflexible determination for what is just and true, while love pervades and binds all. And this is the fruit of the Spirit.

III. Once more, remark the unity of this morality. Men seem to allow that it is possible to be right towards men and wrong towards God. So also they break up the moralities on the human side and act as if a man can be thoroughly corrupt in certain respects, and truly worthy in others. Accordingly men of impure and false lives are received in Society, and their alliances not refused, as if personal vileness and domestic purity can run parallel. Thus, too, office is given to those known to be morally unsound, because it seems to be thought that wickedness is in unconnected parts of character, and public is wholly distinct from private life. But, worst of all, too many instances appear to indicate the notion that piety in the soul is consistent with sharp practice in business. In strongest contrast with this, christianity insists on the oneness of morality. Nowhere in our Lord's teaching, is any distinction made between righteousness toward God, and that toward man. Regeneration is equally effective in divine and human relations. Sin is, of necessity, an unity. If a man be radically wrong towards God, in that self is supremely regarded, how can he be otherwise, toward his fellow beings? So John reasons, and who can gainsay it. Goodness must be equally one, and a man really converted, cannot exhibit the unseemly spectacle of a soul in sections.

IV. Yet again, christian morality is for actual men. Here, the contrast is not with any forms of paganism, but with perversions in christendom itself. Men do not indeed now go into solitudes, as in the early centuries, because they think it difficult to live like christians in society, but are more disposed to remain in society, content not to live like christians. Some even maintain that real christian morals are not for the present, and will only be practicable when Christ's kingdom is fully established on earth. Others, cultivating what they esteem an inward christian life, to the neglect of outward correspondence with it, seem to conceive of the work of the Spirit as removed from daily contacts, and so are little concerned about the strong, homely moralities demanded in those contacts. It may be pleasant for you, my pious friends, to indulge in what you think is heavenly mindedness. But every-day life is famishing for the greatest possible goodness. Heavenly minded people are very much needed in families. Humility is greatly wanted to settle difficulties. Men not easily affronted, are hard to find; and love that only comes from deep experience of the grace of God, is an absolute necessity in daily complications. But a christianity not thoroughly actual, injures the question between belief and unbelief. A favorite assumption by certain writers is, that the morality taught by Christ as characteristic of the kingdom which he established, has been essentially modified on the part of christendom. No doubt christian morals, fully practised according to our Lord's plain intention, would produce changes startling to think of. To act completely in the spirit of christianity, and resolutely apply its ideas and law to our whole conduct in society, would demand sacrifices of which we are now incapable. Still it is insisted upon, that christian morals alone are suited to earth. Our Lord unmistakably claimed this. Himself lived here a human life which he meant men to follow, and plainly showed what he thought was fitted to man on earth. He made so full an exhibition of true morality, that we can judge whether or no it is adapted to all human relations. He taught his disciples to preach this same morality everywhere, and so they never qualified the word committed to them, either in fastidious Greek cities or in impracticable Rome. But we can form some judgment on this question, by considering the fitness of other than christian morality to this world. Certainly everything conceivable of moral systems and standards, except complete, original, christian morals, has been tried. And there is a kind of painful satisfaction in pointing those who object to christian morals as Utopian, to the results of these trials. Review all history, all conduct of State and business, and social intercourse. See how so called practical men have managed human society without christianity, or with its perversions, or stinted measures of its morality. They who would temper the gospel with "enough of the world, the flesh, and the devil," a good deal of Machiavelli, and a modicum of the sermon on the mount, to make a mixture sufficiently practical for the consent of society, surely have little reason for complacency. Behold these continual wars, these overturnings of governments, this antagonism of classes, these destructive competitions, these crises in business; with sorrows for honest men, and crimes for dishonest ones, and temptations for all; this frightful proportion of personal ruins, this great mass of humanity surging along with shocks and manifold wrecks; all directed by shrewd men who smile at christian morality being the rule of actual conduct, and that because it is not practical. They have not tried full christianity. Suppose they do! Does it need much to prove that justice and benevolence are particularly fitted to adjust human affairs, and that society can only fulfill its idea when it receives the morality which Christ taught? To be like Christ is, indeed, to be fitted for heaven, but it is because of being fitted for earth. And this morality, christianity seeks to produce by supernatural provision and influence. A living faith in Christ, identifies man with him. Guilt is removed and the soul brought into right relations to God. Under the divine energy of the Spirit, by the word of God and the discipline of Providence, this moral character is formed. Our judgment of christianity should be determined by this aspect of it. By this we should test its various modifications. As one wanders in Rome, with recollections of the old worship, he sees continually, characteristics of paganism glaring out from beneath the christian surface, and he is impressed with startling evidence, that as in ancient, so in modern Romanism, morality has no necessary connection with religiousness, and that devotion, dirt, and deviltry can keep company together. In Protestant christendom, other forms of this unnatural separation show themselves, and men become formal, or confident in belief, or fervid in emotion, or zealous in works, and yet remain unchanged in moral character. Each type of our church life, in its own way repeats this. It is the old nature reasserting itself in sin, untouched at all, or but slightly, by grace. It is all the worse that men can deceive themselves more easily than others. But after all, nature, though it can be changed, cannot be cheated, and the Jacobs of earth will betray themselves by their purring voices though they wear the furry hands of Esau. There is but one sufficient test for all this; christian morality. There only is the Spirit, where are the fruits of the Spirit. This is the true criterion by which to judge the past and the present of our faith—its epochs, its revivals, its declensions, its every form in which doctrine has been taught or devotion expressed. Hence the statement that the whole question of christianity largely concerns the moral side of human nature. Thus as regards believing: plainly our Lord considered that in certain moral states, men were not likely to believe in him, and that certain other states were the favorable condition for receiving him. Nor is it difficult to see this in the very nature of things. Jesus Christ is indeed absolutely what he is revealed, yet in respect to his being apprehended by men, he is the most relative of objects. To be seen fully as Saviour, he must be seen in relation to sinners. A dark ground of guilt and sin is needed to present him really to the human mind. Where there is no recognition of guilt, no consciousness of sin, what correspondence to a deliverer from guilt and sin can work in the perception of Christ. A man thoroughly sensual is not in a state to judge the person and work of a spiritual Saviour; no more is one coldly intellectual, whether engrossed in physical investigations, metaphysical speculations, or esthetical studies; for he may employ intellect so as to injure his sensibility to moral distinctions, and come to be slightly, if at all, conscious of moral wants. Such a one, by law of compensation, may rise above all low excess into a region of godless thought, where self, exaggerated into monstrous proportions, shall be more antagonistic to the very idea of Christ than lust, or murder, or ambition, or avarice. The question of belief in our day, turns very largely on this. Of course it is easier to see that after a man believes, it depends on his moral state, how much insight he shall have into the innermost character and work of Christ. Actual human nature in the individual, or society, is, to a certain extent, attracted to christianity. Yet it is repelled by the aversion of a selfish will to what demands the dethronement of that selfish will. Very humiliating, but it cannot be denied. Men will make a christendom of their own, or they will be indifferent, or they will crush out the faith entirely if they can. Conscience then is of great account, in all stages of belief in christianity. Men must be convinced of sin, to apprehend the real Christ. They must feel the need of salvation before they will seek the Saviour. A proportionate life in the conscience is necessary for every step in christian progress. Before the greater knowing the doctrine of Christ, must be the greater doing of his will. So in questions of duty. For example, that concerning the particular field of labor for Christ. How are men to perceive the obligation which is imposed by his great command, or how sufficiently understand the real nature of the kingdom he has established on earth, with consciences not up to the moral standard of that kingdom? Evidently something more is needed than a vague, impulsive "call." A clearer view of obligation can only be had, when conscience has increased powers of discrimination. It is the want of this greater moral sensibility, that must be recognized. But so far from accepting this fact of conscience needing cultivation, in order to know our duty, we are apt to think that one's actual conscience is well enough, and it is sufficient to use it as it is, in looking at the gravest questions of duty. It is true that to obtain outward liberty for conscience, cost much, and this is the especial glory of our beloved little State. The consciences of the present generation are very much soothed by historical recollections, elaborate and frequent, of what their ancestors suffered from the wicked old Bay State. And from appearances may we not expect that as works of supererogation for scanty sinners, the heroic persistency of the fathers, will for a long time to come, constitute a stock for consciences in Rhode Island to draw upon. But there must be responsibility beyond the actual conscience, else any amount of impunity, and other moral confusion would follow. Now to avoid certain psychological questions, and not to dwell on analogies in nature, where truths are valid, despite of sincere convictions to the contrary, the effect of regarding the conscience at any given moment as sufficient authority if followed, must be injurious to christian morals. Men, of course, will be satisfied with themselves so long as their consciences do not reprove them. Now how many men are in fact reproved by their consciences to any considerable extent? Some one has said "Men suffer more from their livers, than their consciences" and certainly it looks so. Men are addressed frequently as if they needed quiet to their consciences, when the chief hindrance to their moral improvement, is that their consciences are too quiet already. Recall how our Lord discriminates between men, according to this, and plainly shows that he regards unawakened consciences as prevailing in those about him. The Old Testament describes under different terms, human nature as largely characterized by this state. .Universal history, too, reads like this, granting the saying, "that men knew better than they acted," yet upon the whole, the ancients appear satisfied with themselves. As intellectually they were not apt to be conscious of deficiencies, so morally they were not remarkable for being conscious of their sins. When Socrates began his career, under a full impression of his own ignorance and that of others, he was so struck with the universal self-conceit, that he based his scheme of sounder philosophy on first producing a thorough consciousness of ignorance. You know the result. Men did not wish to know that they did not know; mortified vanity, the most unforgiving of passions, largely helped to put Socrates to death. We have no evidence, despite of what the poets wrote about "The Furies" that the ancient Greeks were much troubled by their consciences. From the pages of the most gifted Latin bard, himself highly redolent of epicureanism, we naturally conclude, that sinners in Rome, must have had an easy time, so far as conscience was concerned. Very striking indeed, the illustration of this when an imperial sinner, great arch-actor of his time, died with self-complacent mockery on his lips. Even those denounced most unsparingly by Rome's stern annalist do not show much moral sensibility in suffering the consequences of their crimes. The same conclusion follows from later history, and we find no marked proofs of disturbing conscience in the Borgias and other lordly wretches of Italy. In days of Spanish cruelty, the good Las Casas testifies sadly to men's satisfaction with themselves, while committing the most shocking crimes. Conscience, apparently, was not very active in France, at court, during the Regency, nor was it in England under the third Stuart, when woman's virtue and man's honor were cheapest. Coming down later, we see little sense of sin in the personages figuring in the reigns of the first Georges of England. The death-bed of one of that line, is a psychological curiosity of its kind. How much did the great Napoleon suffer from conscience? He might possibly have shed a Plutonian tear at the sight of a dog watching by a dead soldier, but what part did conscience have in his grand organization, commensurate with his unceasing lies, his slaughter of millions, and his transcendant self-conceit? We refer his next New England biographer to his now published correspondence for a full exhibition of Napoleon's moral sense. We are apt to claim that our days are better in this respect, still we do not see wrong doers disturbed enough by sense of sin, to effect the statement of a very prevalent moral insensibility. Upon the whole, sinners may be said to be rare, if we consider the opinion entertained of themselves, by different classes of transgressors. These certainly do not appear to have very accusing consciences. On the part of unscrupulous speculators and fraudulent evaders of debt, and heartless epicures, there are no such manifestations of suffering as to deter others. On the contrary, they find no lack of imitators. Look where you will, men are unmistakably sinners, yet without a corresponding sense of sin. If they had it, they could not conceal it. Of course the conditions of a state of probation and education, demand that men be capable of rendering conscience more or less insensible, as well as of cultivating its sensibility. But the ground fact remains, and no popular sophism, nor rhetorical assertion should prevent our clear view of what the actual conscience is, and its bearing on the christianity to be preached. For how can its substance be promoted if this most vital instrument, the moral sense, be not fully apprehended? Then we are prepared to see that to a very great extent we are responsible for the state of our conscience, and that this highest and most delicate sense depends for its due exercise, on its appropriate culture. For indeed we can notice that many influences work to injure its power of discrimination. We are not necessarily conscious when our moral sense is losing this ability to discriminate truly. On the contrary, we account for deterioration in our moral judgments, in ways that wholly ignore any deterioration. We are quick enough to notice the weakening of other powers. We never fail to seek remedies. We change our place for a cold, and cross the ocean for a pain. A slight derangement of our digestion will send us to be tortured and drenched. A torpid liver is alarming, and a slight touch of paralysis will scare any one. When memory fails, how soon we perceive it and are ready to practice mnemonics. We even distrust our judgments at seventy. But what are sickly organs and failing intellect to a man's conscience giving way? And this is far too common. For who can doubt that there are many more with dull moral sense, than with feeble digestion, and where one person is under treatment for limbs, and lungs, and brains, scores might better be, if possible, for ailing consciences. But who is quick to perceive when his sensibility to right is weakened? Who suspects that his conscience is not as quick to see wrong in himself, as it once was? Who becomes afraid that he is growing meaner, or more penurious, or prodigal in self-indulgence, or more ambitious, or more selfish generally, and less comfortable to live with, less to be depended on, his self-conceit increasing, and his moral fibre dissolving? all this, without knowing it. And who leaves a place or an office on account of his moral tone being lowered? And whom have we known travelling to restore an enfeebled moral sense? How many men did you ever meet, seriously alarmed because they remarked that they always felt themselves right? In our day, people change their churches chiefly for social reasons, to be in ecclesiastical harmony with exotic growth of families, sometimes for doctrines, emotion, esthetical gratification, intellectual tastes, and other motives. But who because his conscience was not troubled in a wholesome way? Among many expressing their fears of various diseases, would it not sound strange to hear in like manner, different men anxious about the state of their consciences? Here a tradesman, quite concerned lest his business was dulling his sense of right; Here a lawyer, beginning to question if his special pleading was not qualifying his ability to distinguish between right and wrong; There a physician while solemnly, with nods of indescribable wisdom, he prescribed for "the shocks that flesh is heir to," becoming afraid that the moral function in his own system was not rightly discharged and that he could not trust the diagnosis of his own moral state. Or suppose a minister increasing in power of statement and various perfunctory work, and more able to draw the drifting people, beginning to feel a disagreeable sensation, which makes him doubtful if his conscience be in the best condition to see the pure right, especially when with grave Presbytery or Council ready to confirm him in belief of a heavenly call, and remarkable indications of Providence in larger field, more important congregation, and corresponding provision for the flesh, he goes in a direction whose moral grade is easy to go in, and considerably away from that great command so imperfectly heard by any of us. Or, to make one more supposition, not unnaturally suggested by this occasion. What if a young man who, after some deliberation, has "felt no call" to bear the gospel to the heathen, but is quite sensitive to one from a very inviting parish, should find himself more than suspecting that the true "call" was not some mystical impression, or overpowering attraction, but a strong sense of obligation to obey the fullest sense of Christ's great command, and that duty to feel that obligation, demanded a moral sense of quickest sensibility and moral dispositions in truest harmony with Christ's love for men, then further, what if he should see reason to fear that his actual conscience was not in the fittest state to guide his judgment and his moral dispositions, not in sufficient likeness to Christ for due enlightenment of his understanding, still more what if it became plain to him that he had not cultivated his conscience in college, else perhaps his conclusion about a field of duty had been different. For who can tell what powerful effects on all questions of duty an increased moral sensibility would have, and especially on the duty to preach Christ where he had never been known. Only imagine this quickening of conscience. What a time there would be! Why did not the weird seer of New England imagine such? He might have given the fullest scope to his genius, and made men look deeper into themselves, than he has ever done. Who can say what might be our state here, if such a far within quickening of the conscience were to come upon us, and its painful thrill disturb our self-complacency, and we had to doubt the infallibility of our self-approval. And yet why ought not this to be? For think how far we are below the standard of right, and how sure we are in specific cases to judge ourselves according to our own selfish notions. But for such an awakening of consciences to take place in the present state of society, would be very alarming. The whole aspect of things were changed. Nay, even such a congregation as this might find itself in a great amazement at his real self. This old historic church would never have witnessed such phenomena. How we should go home in sober, painful self-distrust, and review our judgments and decisions and see our conduct and characters in a new light. But let none be disturbed: nothing like this is in danger of happening. It is only fancy. We rest too secure in our actual consciences. Human self-conceit is too profound. Men have not conscience enough to suspect their consciences. Responsibility for the state of our conscience, needs another Butler to take up the theme and treat it philosophically, and above all, a mighty work of the Holy Spirit, to make it felt practically. As it is, our unconscious sins, though often most fatal hindrances to our own growth, and most troublesome to others, and we fear most offensive to God, are the last to give us concern. Here, then is one bar to real progress in christian morality. Men must be made to feel that they are largely accountable for the condition of their moral sense. Why not? Our actual senses and higher powers direct us, but to an indefinite extent our senses and higher powers are what we make them. So our wants determine our procedures, but we are largely responsible for the constraint of our wants, since their strength depends on our cultivation of them. Then, plainly, no small part of the preacher's work in the world, is to educate the conscience itself, to bring it up into the high sphere where it must breathe the pure air of the perfect and eternal right. Surely in the best communities the average conscience does not warrant expectations of highest moral results. Does the promise of the Spirit excuse neglect of culture of the conscience? What else in many cases, is to be expected than surface convictions and sentimental piety that often only varnishes over weak and unstable characters? Ah how different were the results of ministries, if they addressed men habituated to cultivate conscience as they do other parts of their nature. There are various reasons why, with all the good in our christian civilization, men are not as morally discriminating and sensitive as they are religious, but it is impossible to deny that one of them is our failure to train the conscience in due proportion. And if in christendom there be this great defect, and a necessity exists for a higher view of the function of conscience and its correspondent culture, to fulfill the original idea of Christ's kingdom, how important that we send the gospel to heathen lands in the fullness of its christian morality, and that men go hence with conceptions of christianity uninjured by any deteriorations at our hands, with discriminations of right undimmed by the atmosphere of our trade, and politics, and letters, and society, with views of the Holy Spirit's work unaffected by lowered standards of regeneration, and with apprehensions of conscience unmixed with contracting limitations of its office, unweakened by confusing notions of its decisions.

For in this goodly frame and constitution of man, the conscience, though not itself moral character, is a mighty instrument in forming character, and the Holy Spirit greatly employs it. Most plainly is it intended to hold a very important place in the economy of regeneration, and all things groan and travail till it regain its function. Mirror of the everlasting law, it is meant to anticipate the judgments of eternity, and to reflect into the soul, the searchings of divine commands. Oh beauty is a joy, and utility is a good, and knowledge is a help, and thought is a luxury. Say not, we fail to appreciate them and give them due rank in man's composite structure. But above all them, is this great sense of the moral nature. It is itself the highest intelligence, and waits to seal in the light of the Spirit, with complete insight and approval, the various conduct of man, or to echo the divine reproof on human character. So should we seek to rise ourselves, above these low averages of morality, and leave our unworthy standards for the ideal of Christlike, moral excellence, ever striving after clearer conceptions of goodness, till humble and full of awe, our souls shall hunger and thirst after likeness to Christ, and life itself become one continuous aspiration for the Holy Spirit to produce in us the fruitage of every christian virtue.

" Whatsoever things are true!
 Whatsoever things are honest!
 Whatsoever things are pure!
 Whatsoever things are of good report!
 If there be any virtue! If there be any praise!
  think on these things."

THE STATE.

(Delivered before one of the Literary Societies of Brown University, 1862.)

THERE seems no choice of themes at this time. One overmastering thought constrains us, and letters must be subordinate in the scholar's mind to that whose idea is essential to the completeness of all letters and philosophy and religion itself. For God himself, in a very terrible way, is educating us up to the doctrine and appreciation of that noblest form and fruit of society—THE STATE. Whatever it was needful to think and do for individual development, now plainly, since by great exigencies we are forced to act, is it reverential to think in the direction of the whole. Indeed, the divine method proceeds in large part by unities, and doubtless one significance of this moment in our history is a recoil from individualism and a vindication of social unity. We are obeying a mighty conservative instinct to preserve and confirm the State. Better, certainly, is it to pray for it, and die for it—but it is also well to think it out, and enunciate it in high places.

So, then, the State is not a soulless aggregate of individuals, but is itself a noble Life, and we are living in it and out from it. This day we are not so many men and women with names, baptized or unbaptized, fools or wise, workers or lazy, only; not so many members of families or of colleges merely, not even born only in the State of Rhode Island and Providence Plantations. No, thank God, we are participants of a higher National Existence. Its larger, deeper pulsations throb within us. Ours is this lofty State consciousness, becoming more distinct, and, please Heaven! we do not mean to part with it, come what may. This is the moment for us to be in sympathy with the worthiest minds of every age upon this grand theme, from the great Athenian downward, and, with John Milton, to conceive of the State as of "one huge Christian Personage, one mighty growth and stature of an honest man, as big and compact in virtue as in body."

It is a great thing, and worth great sacrifices, to attain the full conception of this. With a comprehension enlarged by the views opening upon us, and made more luminous by their contrasts; with an earnestness becoming more intense through the tragic realities of this hour, let us then apprehend it, First, as directly authorized in its origin, alike by the revealed word and the natural law of God, not as asking leave to be, through some supererogatory compact of men; but through a certain divine necessity working in the constitution of things, whereby society must crystallize into State forms. Scope enough is left for the human will to act in all responsibility, yet with no exception in the highest of all spheres—the moral—allowed to mar the universal order, but anarchy made as impossible as chaos; and this from honest rudiments, up to most complete political organization, manifested as a condition of social being, into which men come without being committed as to whether they agree to be governed, any more than whether they agree to be born at all. Secondly, Set before the mind the substance and functions of the State. Its substance is summarily government; legislative, in that it enacts laws out of existing obligations; judicial, in that it discriminates according to those laws; and executive, in that it secures the observance of law. Then its functions—How high are these? Towards God, it is, whether expressed or not, the mightiest illustration of the Supreme Divine State in which men exist. All our great ideas need to be educated; and this most comprehensive one, that we are subjects of God's moral government, is taught us through the ages by the State. For, notice how it makes us familiar with intelligent will, moving and controlling immense activities, and inculcates upon us, through the compression of our swollen individuality, and the suggestion of our accountability to administered law, that we were formed to be under government, and that true liberty is harmony with law.

But the functions of the State towards men is the aspect most immediately concerning us. Observe how various and essential this is. It restrains, ever so gently or violently, with consciousness or unconsciousness on our part. Oh, what would not men do and be but for this restraining force! Again, it protects. Think how the State guards us! Asleep or awake, we are within its outstretched arms, and its watchful eye is ever upon us and ours. Abroad, its mere touch on wax acts like a talisman, and means fleets and armies, if the solitary traveller be injured, as it says, "Take heed what thou doest, for this man is a Roman." Once more, consider its energy in developing the individual. Its compacted membership, and its organic life, like the action of a harmonious body upon the smallest part, tend to start and sustain all growth. What were man outside of the State? Wherever, by some extraordinary circumstance, he is found in a condition approaching this, he presents the most humiliating phenomena of partial, inferior, nay, stagnant humanity. The animal, or rather the vegetable, predominates in him. But as the vine stock supplies each leaf with juice to fill out its own proportion, so the mighty unity of the State communicates its life to each of us ; and our own identity is more distinct, because of this very derived vigor.

The topic which interests us most is, however, the Form of the State. Here, mark how the utmost variety of this is consistent with integrity of origin and substance. The State is too much a creature of God not to be capable of a wide range of modification. In this it must resemble all parts of nature where substantial properties remain through very great changes in outward conditions, and where utility and beauty depend to a great extent on this combination. So is it like art and all mind, and home. So it agrees with the church, which sublimely rebukes all attempts to confine its divine identity within any form, by its manifestation of Christian doctrine and life in so many organizations ; and forbids the assertion of immunity from heresy and sin by a painfully suggestive history common to all. In a word it is like man himself, who can repeat almost endlessly types of human nature, and yet remain identical. So far, then, from committing the divine idea of the State to the narrow mould of one form, and thus contradicting all analogies of creation and Providence, as well as opposing it to all growth of man, the true conception of the State, as Divine, is that which meets all possible exigencies of society, by variety of forms. And this view is confirmed when we consider the manner in which such variety occurs. Thus, a change in the form of the State may be brought about by an imperceptible process going on like some of the processes in nature, or in human opinion. This were the highest conceivable mode, and one which might wholly prevail, were there no inward disturbing elements. Something of this, indeed, we can trace in the histories of States, in which, without violence, and even insensibly, the form has changed. Yet another mode is that of constitutional changes, where, with more or less agitation, and under different motives, the acting government conducts its own modification. This, too, is more honorable to human nature, and we have illustrations enough of this in history to show what extremes might be avoided. Then comes the last and exhaustive mode—Revolution—in which, with more or less violence, and on right or wrong occasions, men avail themselves of the final prerogative in moral beings to obey God rather than man, and under peril of condemnation, if they mistake duty, accept the alternatives of a struggle, and change the form into what the exigencies of society demand. This, alas, is the more common mode, and is a humiliating comment on the inability of man to develop harmoniously. But even revolution leaves intact the sacredness of the State. Nay, it is a homage paid by human nature in its wildest movement, to government, in that it invokes supremest right, and is an appeal from wrongs and infractions of obligation to the majesty of law. And this, not with the self-complacent notion that sincerity makes truth and a higher law, and so releases from wrong the simply honest revolutionist; but with solemn acceptance of the same condition which guards truth in the physical domain, where men have to act in the certainty that God holds them under penalty of explosion, and poisons, and all sorts of evil consequences, not to what they *think*, but to what *is* true.

Thus far, all concerns the form, and touches not the substance of the State. As yet there is no such self-assertion as, that men originate their duty to obey, continue it by a perpetually recurring consent, and make it cease by an arbitrary act of will. The aberrations thus far are within defined limits. We conceive of these modes as in the sphere of State transformation, and however much room there is in them for hopeful and sad material of history, we still remain at a wide remove from the abyss where that which Pluto held in pure reason, and Paul magnified by the inspiration of the Holy Ghost, perishes in the infernal negation of government by Secession. This, then, is the doctrine of the State which we believe is forming into intelligent conception, through the resistless logic of events, forcing us upon high ground.

That our actual State is Democratic, affects not the strength of the idea. Let others hold it under forms of autocracy, or of constitutional monarchy. We were shaped into this form of Democracy by a process as rigid and sovereign as that which is represented in forming planets out of star dust. We grew into it as plants grow; for our roots run down deep and wide into a historic past. Nay, to fulfill all analogies, we were born in due time. We early asserted our national life, not from the deliberating inventions of men, but the necessities of elements working beneath and within all conventions, compelling them to act. The ease and naturalness with which the government entered upon an announced and fully conscious existence, is as sufficient a proof of national life, as the jointed limbs and intending mind are of a living man. The State stood up, one great personality, instinct with organic, pervading energy, and not a company of merchants banded for traffic, nor a ship's crew gathered for a voyage. It took its place among the governments of earth, itself a myriad crowned Democracy among monarchies and empires, challenging recognition, arrogant, if you will, ofttimes wicked, as other States, yet not without some sense of God; in all respects, a State, with the consciousness, not of parts, but of a whole, its citizens abroad looking up not to pelican and rattle-snake banners, but to yon broad ensign, floating as far and proudly as the red cross of England. Thus has it continued, hardened into unity by the lapse and the conflicts of time. The agony of this moment shows that deeper than mere sentiment, or any conviction of interest, the instinct of a national existence has been roused, and merges all questions in its vast vitality. These later movements, resembling in their fearful earnestness the determined purpose of France in her darkest hour, to maintain her unity, are the involuntary proofs of an increasing horror at the unnaturalness, as well as the wickedness of dismemberment. No! by the tumultuous feelings which struggle in us, and which I dare not analyze, by all the glorious past, and the ominous future, this government passes not away as a shape of air. No palmetto rod tipped with ebony can dissolve it in magic quiet. No conjuror's mouth can utter a spell mighty enough to resolve harmoniously the mystic numbers of the State. If it perish, it perishes like giant Rome, limb torn from limb, of one great body. So, then, we are shut up to this actual American Democracy, as the State whose idea we must cherish, and whose history we must accomplish, something, indeed, capable of disastrous end, but also of glorious possibilities something for the scholar and

Christian to dwell upon and honor, something to pray and fight for, something to live and die for!

And this form of the State is now subjected to perilous trial. At such a time, while the largest thoughts and the noblest impulses will hold us firm to our conclusions, there are narrower aspects and baser feelings which will work in us to weaken them. Let us consider some of these side views. Here, as in everything human, we must proceed by comparison. There is a choice between sinners, is after all the utmost we can affirm of men. Before God we will indeed confess. Not to him will we utter any thing but humblest acknowledgments of our abuse of his goodness, of our failure to fulfill the magnificent destiny He traced for us. Not even in face of our own ideal, will we deny our grievous defects. But when other national sinners make us the subject of a homily on the faults of democracy we lift our heads and challenge their judgment. Shall France exult over us? or her Guizot use us to point the moral of his next pamphlet on this theme? At what awful expense to the highest civilization has she attained glory and the power of corrupting Europe at will? Dare she to-morrow disband only a few myriads of her soldiers, and trust civil order and "Mon Empereur" to the people? Does she present the fairest conception of the State? Ah, let her St. Hilaires tell us the profound hurt of France, where unteachable Bourbons and impracticable reformers wait the moment of convulsion. Shall Austria lecture us on the blessings of Imperialism, and illustrates its superiority by the benefits to society of the Hapsburgs? Or must we save all our humility for England's reproof? listen reverently to Lord Brougham's last chapter of his political philosophy, composed in his peerage and dotage both, and accept English glorification of the British Empire as the best illustration of the State? We will not review her distant past. But what are her national results, to justify her Alison's and Blackwood's assumptions of superiority? It is not a question now of her achievements in arts, and other civilization, upon English soil; nor of what her citizens have accomplished for the world's evangelization. Nothing shall provoke us to forget these; but we are on trial in the world's history; our present impugners are our own monarchical and aristocratic kindred; and we must rightly compare the faults of States, ere we confess Democracy a failure, and Democrats sinners above others. What has she to say for her foreign relations? When has that meteor flag ceased to wave in quarrel with some other nation? What great principle of right has she ever warred to maintain? For what high purpose has she kept up her costly armaments? Let the judgment of Europe answer, if she does not set more store by her calico than by the rights of other people. Has Napoleon's estimate of her foreign policy been proved to be harsh? and what alternative have we from De Tocqueville's severe philosophy of England's international morality? Do her eulogists forget that the same age has seen her holding up Bonaparte as the very Devil, battling him to the death for great ideas, and then bowing reverently at his tomb in company with Mephistopheles, his nephew, under a deep conviction of power? Let John Chinaman testify whether she puts justice above the price of drugs. And when she lifts her voice, and cants worse than any conventicle about the aggressive spirit of Democratic States, let India say if the wild Northman blood which flows in us from her, has not urged the English State to conquests which our Democracy never dreamed of. Thus much for England abroad. If it be the necessary outworking of her inward State-life, so much then is there to abate her boasting over others. But what of that inward life? What changes quite on the verge of revolution? Despite her vaunted system of checks, she could not pass her corn laws without making Peers faster than they were born. What is that condition of things which makes her fear convulsion when a foreign crop fails? And what that constitution of society, where the soil is so disposed of that it cannot feed its own children? But what has the State done for the people? With unequalled resources, how much has she effected in the elevation of her masses? Her pauper list is astounding; her criminal register affrights her own officials; and her plethoric establishment is embedded in a population whose lowest strata are hard upon heathenesse. Save for emigration, and that to the very land whose institutions she disparages, what had been the history, ere this, of the English State? Oh, with what feelings must Americans regard England! We would love her, if she would let us; for she is our mother country. Her blood flows in our veins. Her very names are ours; her language and her Christianity. We did not ask her arms or money; but, one word of sympathy with us, in this crisis of our history, had bound us to her forever. Yes, most various are the emotions with which we look at the different aspects of England. Land of lordly pride and priestly arrogance; yet of intelligent and determined freemen! Land of scholars; yet of brutal ignorance! Land where abounds every grace that illustrates Christianity; yet where rank and foul irreligion riots in masses of humanity! Land of gentlemen, whose language and bearing make us proud of our race; and yet of boors, whose degradation might shame us of our species! Land of conflict and triumph too, of constitutional liberty, firm when other nations are rocking; and agitating reform when others are stagnant. Land of our Fathers, that gave us all we have in church and State and home, all liberty, all high inspirations, all great works of mind and heart, and with them the curse of mammon and slavery, too! Seen from one point of view, behold Britannia, a majestic form, serene with intelligence, the dispenser of Christian civilization to subject millions. We look again, and lo! a hideous figure, the hugest incarnation of Pharisaism, a crowned Tartuffe among the nations, her conscience torpid with opium, her hearing stopped with cotton, and her homilies on forbearance choking with the blood of tortured Sepoys! No, we cannot see that other forms present the State in such comparison as to authorize any affectation of superiority on their part. What has the past proved? Alison wrote ten weary volumes in special plea against Democracy. He meant to show that its inherent badness was such, that it could not worthily develop the State. He ends with the conclusion which his country's catechism might have taught him; and in his closing chapter dares not affirm any thing more than that the sin in human nature will spoil any form of government—a very safe assertion, and tolerably modest for a Scotch tory, in review of the troubles which kings and nobles have made in the British islands during their whole history; to say nothing of Europe and the rest of mankind. This, we admit painfully, of our mode of making real the State. We are learning more of that sin every day, but then it is only Democratic so far as to be identical, while the largest part is human and especially Anglo-Saxon.

There is something singularly unfair in the way in which writers treat this question. They strangely omit to draw even fair inferences from the unworthy exhibition of the State by other forms, while the failure of the Democratic has been judged in advance. Thus what injustice has been done to ancient Athens! But Grote has shown with an exactness which every scholar must prize, and a comprehensiveness and fairness worthy of the historic spirit, that she, of all Greece, rendered best the idea of the State. The truest conception of the public, the greatest reverence for law, were really found in her Democracy. And now, when this great hour of trial brings out a humiliating distrust of the State as constituted here, and men express doubt of its form, it becomes us to recognize what results of the State have been accomplished during its life of near a century. It is difficult to bear with some among us, who utter their Jeremiads, not against evil in all governments, but our monopoly of it; and this directly in the face of wondrous benefits. Why dwell on them? Can any man who has travelled to any purpose besides pictures and French cookery, or who reads and thinks beyond his small circle of reactionists, fail to see them? Protection to life and property, the well-being of millions, the large provisions of education, the happiness and purity of homes, the great ends of justice answered, the quiet of honest industry, the peaceful tenor of personal tastes and civil order not jostled even by the tread of armed men, and the church of Christ stronger this hour in the hearts of the people than if upheld by the arm of power. May we not refer to a fair proportion of character nurtured in this Democracy? If it has produced demagogues like other countries, yet has it not also had statesmen the peers of any foreign land? If it has brought forth as shallow ignoramuses and self-conceited pretenders as those who disgrace European letters, has it not also developed genuine scholars and humble thinkers? If it has its knaves in business, and unscrupulous speculators and repudiators of honest debts, to join in shameful fellowship with commercial dishonesty abroad, yet has it not also merchants of as pure integrity, and as incapable of base traffic, as any across the water? If the bones of American slave-traders pollute the soil of Africa, awaiting resurrection along with men-stealers from Liverpool, yet there too have fallen holy souls, whose sacrifice rises like fragrant incense, and joins, before the throne of God, the offerings of precious lives from England! Do other forms of the State boast of peculiar loyalty to a reigning person? Yet the State here has developed loyalty to itself, something deeper than personal reverence, an instinct of deference to existing authority, something higher than sentiment, a principle of obedience to law, the rich and poor rising to maintain government, and with the past thrilling them, meaning to maintain it at every cost. Surely, these are fair fruits of the State! Nor has any thing occurred in this present exigency which might not have happened in any other form. The species of ambitious men who would rather reign in hell than serve in heaven, is not peculiar to democratic institutions. If slavery be a fruitful source of trouble here, so might it be in any government. * If the local independence of parts of the country, as expressed in the theory of extravagant State rights, the practice of secession, against which some provision was made, which, years ago, De Tocqueville pointed out, and of whose danger our noblest fathers warned us, has at last, after divers manifestations, swollen into this monstrous self-assertion, under the fever heat of slavery, and is the real peril of this hour; yet this, too, is not the especial defect of Democracy. It has been, and is, fruitful in other forms. How long was Great Britian in consolidating her unity? Nay, it is not secure yet. Witness the necessity of transplanting the Celtic Irish, and colonizing Ireland from England and Scotland. It was longer yet before the boasted unity of France was complete; and the terrible chapter of La Vendee is yet recent. Recall the war of the Sunderbund in Switzerland—the struggle nearest like ours, and full of instruction how soonest to end it. Spain has had her experience; Germany must do something more than *sing* " Ein Deutschland" before she becomes so; and Italy, too, even after the solemn vote and bloody welding together of her beautiful provinces, must overcome various repulsions ere she grows into one kingdom. No! this is something common to all governments. We are at one of those points in a nation's history which all must reach, when the elements are either to settle into firmer compactness, or disintegrate more entirely.

Doubtless the question is made more difficult by slavery; but the issue turns on the inward force of the State to fuse these elements. Our fathers tried to spare us this crisis; but it has come upon us, and we must meet it. But when, in comparison with other governments, men distinguish this as endangered, we look out on this actual earth, and wonder at this peculiar distrust. For this Democratic State is not the only one to dread the future! Will Germany shape quietly into the grand development her philosophers and scholars write out for her? Shall the French Empire peacefully descend to the little Zouave who now plays in the Tuileries? Has the future no terrors for England? When the good Victoria sleeps with her fathers, can no contingencies arise? Will John Bull endure to the end such expense for German blood? Believe you he will sing " God save the King," and pay his debts for another George the Fourth? The future! ah, perhaps the world will not last long. Monarchies, democracy, hierarchies and all may vanish from the wearied scene of human wickedness and folly. But if Providence should not accept the suggestions of Dr. Cumming and his impatient folk on the eschatology, any more than it consulted Ptolemy on the creation of the world, and conclude not to burn up yet this magnificent earth; if long ages of history are yet to come, and many an humbling lesson is to be given to national pride that this conceit may be taken out of men, who can tell what form of government shall suffer most before humanity develop out the noblest idea of the State? Into that future we look tremblingly, as becometh those who believe in the fearful scope of the human will above and within material forces, in the moral government of God, and his clearly manifested mode of redeeming through suffering. But we look hopefully, too, because we believe in great truths to be vindicated, and in great blessings to come through chastisements. But we do not see how we can improve the prospects of the State in the future, by any change of forms, since God is plainly rebuking men in them all.

Besides, if we take the counsel of European advisers and

try a king, whom shall we send for? Bomba,—he is without charge, and doubtless would listen to a call; but I question if the parish would agree upon him. The kindly Alexander has at present his hands full of the slave matter, and we would rather wait to see how he manages that which our autocrats on both sides cannot dispose of. Shall it be the great Adroit on the French throne? Ah! some of the American clergy might have accepted the uncle, but I query if many could be found to consent to the nephew, with his "Ideas Napoleonic." Shall we import from England? Ah! not one word of disrespect for the queenly English wife and mother. All honor to her for whom Americans will pray, "God save her," as truly as her own subjects; but then I fear the farmers would not be willing to support all the Coburgs.

A far different question, however, is that which concerns the place of a higher class in the State. For there must be such and democracy is no exception to this part of social crystallization. Our choice is to determine who shall be the higher class—the *Aristoi;* and indeed very much depends on our settlement of this. An aristocracy of family is not possible. In England, even, they are sadly mixed, and plebeian blood flows widely in aristocratic veins. But here, where we know each other's pedigree with painful accuracy, the confusion is hopeless. The holes of the pit are quite recent from which the most pretentious were digged. Each noble house, unfortunately, like Jonathan Oldbuck's piece of antiquity, has some who "mind the bigging o't." Shall it be an aristocracy of wealth? Yes, rightly, so far as it represents talent that achieved and maintains it; so far as it is employed to refine the taste, improve the manners and bless society. Indeed, it is only justice to honor the rich who generously furnish means to establish a nobler aristocracy than themselves. But let all men judge if in fact the State is furnished with a higher class, worthy of the social needs, by the operations of wealth! Do the mass of our patricians adorn place by gifts of intellect and fine culture and grace of bearing? I will not ask if they have the especial virtues of Christianity; for the world has long since proved that men may be religious without moral goodness, dogmatic without life, and ecclesiastical without being Christian! Do their youth promise the material for eminence? Are they first in scholarly attainments? employing their means for high pursuits? Nay, tell us what constitutes admission to the clubs and drawing-rooms, and alliances of our Belgravias and St. Germains, besides money and lacquer. Alas, for this type of American aristocracy, which Europe scorns; and to whose simian god so many among us sacrifice affection, manhood, and religion itself! How grimly nature, who will accept only reality, smiles at all our arbitrary agreements, and quietly vindicates God's truth. You may entrench dullness ignorance and sensuality within riches; you may call off talent from education, and force bright intellects despoiled of finished discipline into money making; but you cannot thus form a higher class. But shall there be an aristocracy of genuine superiors— the Aristotelian—the true, who shall preside by right of the strongest? Aye! a thousand times aye! with endowments of mind enlarged and quickened and disciplined by thorough training; men raised naturally above the average, and in such proportion as to be a recognized class, not by any prescription, asking no preogatives, but simply taking a higher place by virtue of fitness; from whom may come statesmen and legislators and the professions; and fitting occupants for station; yes, indeed, give us such an aristocracy; for God in his word, and his constitution of society, and in his history of States, teaches us to seek it; something to which men may worthily pay reverence, and young men look up. This, please God! if we get through this struggle a State, we will urge as strongly as the education of the mass; and we will urge it now. For indeed the mass have had great attention to their culture; and nobly have they approved themselves, and vindicated the wisdom of our fathers in establishing this broad basis of public intelligence. Nay, they will vote themselves schools; and let them do so! But the very contrast with the people only enforces our perception of the need of a higher class to accomplish this goodly structure. This is a great want. When we rise above general education, our standard is low. Too much is left to the individual. There is no system to work by even pressure, and elevate any sufficient number, while the instincts of action, and the craving for immediate results, draw the great proportion scantily furnished, into the vortex of public life. Then add to this, the almost despotic influence of business, the easier eminence of wealth, which absorbs so much talent away from study; and how can we escape deficiency in this part? Years ago, the most thoughtful observer of our institutions noted it, and in a philosophical and kindly spirit pointed out its deformity and danger. Is not this deficiency apparent now? We must look at this in severer comparison than may be agreeable to our pride. The completeness of a great State demands an honest sense of any unfaithfulness to its idea.

But it is not uncommon to hear that the people will never appreciate a higher class; that there are already enough of the right men for all eminence; but that they shrink from the arts necessary to win the public. And then it is not unusual to apply to these actually existing, but unappreciated, capacities, certain famous words often repeated with soft unction for neglected souls, about "gems of purest ray in caves of ocean;" and "flowers wasting sweetness on desert air;" and "village Hampdens;" and "mute, inglorious Miltons;" and "guiltless Cromwells."

Now the people cannot help appreciating a higher class if there be one. God made men to look up. They will always have some recognized superiors. The only question is, what their type shall be. When, in history, from Pericles down, did the mass ever refuse to own the leading of superior men? The strongest must conquer; and the infidel's sneer hides in it the Christian's faith. Create such a class, and never fear that the people will not appreciate them. But what of unappreciated worth itself? Did you ever know one of these complainers who did not himself, or his friends for him, use arts sufficient to attract the public? And what of unconscious merit? Are men ordinarily so very modest as to underrate their abilities? Do we educate up to such ideals as awe with a sense of responsibility? What office in church or state requires a bounty to induce, or a draft to compel, acceptance? On the other hand, it remains to be proved that any man can be kept out of his place in this roomy world and exciting country. It is easy to find men unequal to their positions, but very difficult to find any superior to them. The divine order leaves not things so uncertain, or the high qualities of men and their uses unrelated. We may be sure that no gems are lost even in unfathomable caves of ocean; and no traveller of genuine feeling ever saw a flower in the desert, or on the edge of a glacier, who did not thank God for placing it there; or who thought its fragrance wasted. And so with men. If there be any Hampdens in our villages, we may be certain they will find full scope for their talents where they are; and if they be really fit for Congress, they need no caucus nor contracts to send them there. Real Miltons, too, are never mute nor inglorious. When they come, they bring God's warrant of imperishable song; and you need not have any more apprehension that their gifts will be unrecognized, than that the note of the lark, or the flight of the eagle will be mistaken among the myriads of grasshoppers which chirp and skip along our fields. We see no indications of Cromwells in these parts, among those who safely declaim most about him. We have nothing of this kind; the large comprehension, the iron will, the unblenching courage. Our sort are "guiltless," at least, of fight, and only daring on paper. And though doubtless a self-denying ordinance would not be amiss in our parliament, yet who will pass it? Rest quiet; if there be a Cromwell in the land, he will do all his work, and rooms will be ready for him in the White House, if that be his mission. No, it is safer to accept the humbling conclusion that if a higher class do not lead in all the relations of society, it is because we have not such a higher class, and must create it. God indeed must give the brains and blood to form master minds; but we have already given the systems of education which we can enlarge and apply to make the most of average talent, which shall produce those master minds. For we read history to little purpose, if we think these shoot up from uncultivated and fallow soil. In vain we echo Carlyle's cry, and repeat Tennyson's poetry about the "coming man." In vain we catch up each incomplete personage whom some glaring accident, some combination of favorable circumstances, or some prejudice of party in our ever shifting scenes, may have thrust into prominence, without basis of genius or stable acquisitions. This is not the stuff out of which that mysterious individual, "the coming man," is made. Not so works God in history. His Moses and Pericles; his Pauls, and Augustines, and Luthers, come with culture as well as gifts. Not England's money nor her pedigree have made her State; but her higher class, formed of Lords and Commons alike by her schools and universities, have led in arts and arms the industry and energy of the people, up to her present greatness. The forming men in our own early history constituted such a class in the then existing proportions of society; and they who look for men equal to the grave emergencies and ordinary concerns of public life to arise spontaneously from an unprepared soil, ought to have learned better by this time. We hear a great deal of self-made men; but save as all truly educated men are such, let the experience of every department in life answer if self-made men are not poorly made, in every one's judgment but their own. Allowing that genius may dispense with much of the training indispensable to the great average, or rather can appropriate it more entirely and rapidly, yet genius is too rare for society to live by. Meanwhile, the politician hastily extemporized, or merely practised in details of faction, cannot fill the exalted office of the statesman, whose mind has been rendered comprehensive and discriminating by long and generous discipline, and who brings to public affairs the experience of history, and the practise of States. Again, the man who is so little acquainted with the works of older and better thinkers, as to put forth his own crude speculations with the assumption of original thought, and the confidence of ultimate truth, cannot meet those intellectual wants which demand in the highest exercise of mind an exhaustive acquaintance with past philosophy and science. Nor so long as society has needs which create and continue the several professions, can any thing short of a high standard suffice for the worthy idea of the State we are contemplating. What is more humiliating and mischievous than the various caricatures of the physician's noble calling, whose very completeness implies a long and reverential study of nature? And what can take the place in the community of a body of accomplished advocates and jurists? There is no brighter record in history of regard for constitutional freedom than can be shown by the superior class of lawyers. They have withstood alike kingly prerogatives and popular lawlessness, in moments of greatest peril to liberty. Woe indeed to the State, if a low standard in this profession expose it to the assaults of the destructive, and substitute the changing will of the mass for the firm embodiment of justice, and the tranquil voice of law. There is no time now for a worthy plea in behalf of a highly educated ministry. But it is enough to say, that in a country where sacred conventionalisms cannot stand the pressure of actual moral wants, we may be sure that no embryo, partial gifts, no phosphorescent rhetoric, no imperfect culture, can meet the exigencies of truth and faith, which require men trained in severest discipline of mind and heart, who shall not have to go out of their absorbing work for mental stimulus; whose awful idea of pastoral excellence shall keep them engrossed and humble; and whose " Nolo episcopari" in the smallest parish shall be felt as truly as in the largest field of Christendom.

Yes, we admit this great need. Who is there in this hour, when the people are honoring popular education so nobly, but must feel the want of a fitting climax to that education? Who will not comprehend in his idea of the State, this essential part? Surely, this is the place to utter the claims of a higher class of educated men. You will respond to it. Aye, by our conscious defects, let us seek to raise others to a worthier capacity. That great conception of a State, now working out in agony, calls for this at our hands. This is no episode in history, no struggle of an hour; but itself the inevitable development of the past, it is the forming of a vast future. Let us build while we fight. Give those coming years of the Republic a higher class to guide their course and represent their destinies. If sacrifice be demanded, then let it be of men worth the offering; for we live in a world where no great good comes but through sacrifice, whether it be for the salvation of men, or for the redemption of a nation. As there is nothing in the Democratic form of the State which encloses our national life, to forbid the very highest excellence of this part, so may it increase its central force without disturbing its essential structure. The very efforts it puts forth to preserve itself may consolidate the State. Every violent pressure may bind its sections into more substantial unity. Each victory and defeat may weld us together more closely,

The rapid commingling and perpetual confluence of our armies may soften down the distinctions of territorial lines. The government to which we are giving our choicest lives may be cemented anew with our blood, and become the object of exclusive reverence; while the place of its occupancy, guarded so jealously against the foul conspiracy, may win a regard such as Romans had for the Capitol. Amid the many evils of the camp, may not our young men learn more subordination; and if at last this great conflict, after years of suffering, end in the full vindication of government, and the State emerge, worn indeed, humbled but strong, may we not hope from the course of Providence, that all ties of authority will grow stronger, and that in church, and home, and school, and every relation, men will pay more reverence. Nay, with law so terribly magnified, God himself, as He hath done before in analogous circumstances, may visit with His peculiar blessings our people; and in after years, when men tell of the great Secession, they may speak of the great Awakening that followed its rebuke in history.

But of one thing we may be assured, come weal or woe, the State with us must be Democratic. Like it or not, we are shut up to this. The people have the power; they will never give it up. How can we reason differently from the nature of man and the great courses of history? As surely as the man-child comes of age, and takes his property, though he use it badly, so surely must the Demos every where rise to government. They know this abroad. It is only a question of time; and what is that in God's vast periods? Hence the "fear of change perplexes monarchs;" and beneath the confidence with which writers assert the im-

The State.

possibility of the Democratic State, is evident the conviction that to this form society finally tends. But here there is no question of time; no possible alternative. We must work out the problem of the State in Democracy. What its proportions and character—that, indeed, is the tremendous issue with us. If through our selfishness and cowardice, we be proved incapable of the mighty outline so plainly traced out by the Divine architect, and we cannot maintain this unity, then lost to us is the noblest destiny ever offered to man since the doom of God's ancient people. Oh, who wants to live in such a degradation! No great idea of the State, characterizing and pervading all human interests, but every thing diminished and petty; men dwarfed and bitter in sectionalisms; provincial literatures; philosophies narrowed by lines of territory; religion circumscribed by spaces; and communities dashing against each other in endless strifes. Oh, think how those who come after, will curse us! Think how they who shall have waited for our failure, will look on and say, "These men began to build and were not able to finish." But if, rising to the great meaning of this trial, through God's grace we fully meet the emergency and accept but one conclusion—though it cost every thing to reach it—then, indeed, life is worth living. Then we shall complete this noble structure, and the State in majesty and beauty shall fulfill its noblest ends, and be a fitting sphere for every grand conception, for every human and divine concern. Such we believe to be the lesson of this hour,—to elevate the fundamental dogma of the State to its right place in truth and morality. Yes, the State above individuals, as God above all! To this, His great creature, He is training us to give up every thing. No tie of home is too sacred, no interest, nor joy of self is to weigh a moment in comparison. Other questions, indeed, mingle with this; and it may be while this comprehensive one is agitating, they shall be disposed of. If uncontrollable complications force them into issue with national existence, then, as men to save a laboring bark, throw overboard things engaged to be carried, why, overboard with any thing that would save the great ship of State! But now, one overmastering question should rule the hour; no mixed issue, but a grand vital doctrine; no blind, quaking morass of opinions and feelings, but a broad adamantine platform, on which one may stand firm amid factious dictations and dilettanti, declamation and changeful reactions; conscious of truth dear to Almighty God, had in charge by the ages, magnified by the cross of Christ, and vindicated by the eternal judgment. Then raise high to-day the great acclaim of holy love of country. "If I forget thee, O Jerusalem, let my right hand forget her cunning. If I do not remember thee, let my tongue cleave to the roof of my mouth. If I prefer not Jerusalem above my chief joy!"

The Life Hid With Christ in God.

[*Newport, R. I., August 16th, 1857.*]

Colossians III. 3. For ye are dead and your life is hid with Christ in God.

THE Apostle is correcting errors of the Colossians respecting angel worship, and a vain philosophy which depreciated Christ. As is his wont, he utters a truth far more comprehensive than the particular errors concerned, and occupies himself more with the positive work of Christianity, its restoration of the soul, than with the negative, its destruction of sin. Out of the overflowing fullness of its idea, comes this rich statement of Christian life, "ye are dead," he says; "ye are as if dead to the life of sin!" Alike from the nature of moral being, and our own painful experience, we learn that though moral evil is, in one aspect, the absence of good, yet, as known to us, it is much more than this. It manifests itself, by no means negatively, in our world. On the contrary, to use our Lords own illustration, the vegetable life of a tree producing bad fruit, is no more real vegetable life (though bad in itself), than the moral life of a sinner. "Sinning" is real moral life (though sinful in itself). It is believed that the profoundest apprehension and most actual observation, agree in regarding sin as having a very terrible life. The sinner lives out his sins from an inward life of sin. Does not this agree with the deepest experience of men? Nay, does it not express the common view? If sin is only outward, or, if inward, existing there in a lifeless state, why do you *not free yourself from it?* Surely the folly as well as the evil of the thing, is very evident, and becoming more so, as society traverses the ages amid increasing light. We see nothing gained by denying a sinful living nature in man; because, be he in what condition he may, he is a living nature. Nature overpowers all that is overlaid or constrained. It crops out from beneath, upon all surfaces of conduct, and mocks our conventional religion. This life of sin testifies to its energy, by our sense of condemnation, that fearful action of conscience when quickened to discriminate our vices and evil desires, our master passions and self-love. All these disordered relations of man to himself, his God, and his fellows seen in the individual and the whole race, are very palpable fruits of a life deepseated. This life may have considerable unconsciousness of its dangers and wickedness, as when one describing it, says of himself, " I was alive without the law once. I was not conscious of the condemnation or power of sin. I did not feel the exciting influence of the law, my conscience was not sufficiently awake to make me feel my sinfulness." This life without the law is a very common phenomenon in the history of sin. It is one of the conditions of probation that men may become, to a great degree, morally insensible. A large proportion of mankind live in strange self-complacency, and are not troubled about their sins, but even approve things in themselves, which must be wrong in the sight of God. Indeed, no man's moral sense is up to the perception of *the whole law.* So that the soul most advanced in the divine life, whose conscience is most alive to his defective character, will be humbled by this fact, and exclaim in self-abasement. " Who *knoweth his errors!* Cleanse thou me *from secret faults.*" But this life of sin is often attended with considerable consciousness of its danger and wickedness. Our probation includes always more or less of light, and it is the mercy of God that his Holy Spirit does not leave men to the full exercise of their possible self-conceit. Whether they will or no, their consciences are cultivated somewhat and many who wear a very self-satisfied exterior, are, nevertheless, a good deal concerned about themselves, and do not dare to think much. Still more, when the law really comes and identifies itself with the conscience, and speaks through it, then indeed it is impossible to avoid the consciousness of guilt and sinfulness. In this revelation of the soul to itself by the Holy Spirit, the life of sin is necessarily discovered, and even excited to a bad activity. This is one part of "life with the law." The sinner sees himself, feels himself as he is, by an unmistakable sense of condemnation, by the working of his inmost nature out into light. If nothing more came of it, yet were this more fitting than to exist in a perpetual lie, part and parcel of it, himself a lie unto himself. There is then no intoxication of self-righteousness, no sham of soul, in which the moral sense is degraded and paralyzed; but there is something more, and the Apostle appeals to it as the ground of his admonitions. "Ye are dead to this life of sin. Ye have been awakened from its state of unconsciousness. Ye have been made painfully conscious of its guilt and evil nature and are now delivered from it. Henceforth there is no condemnation to you. Freely justified you are no longer regarded as guilty, and may look forward with humble confidence that at the last you will not be treated as a sinner. You are dead to the living power of sin. The life of sin has received its death wound. Considered in regard to the certainty of its final and not remote complete extinction, its evil nature is dead in you. Only a question of time concerns its complete destruction. Though now it struggle and put forth frightful strength, and you have to cry out 'Oh wretched man that I am, who shall deliver me from the body of this death?' yet is it really dead in the great comparisons of your being. These are but its dying convulsions. Your great Deliverer hath as effectually conquered sin in itself as in its consequences." Thus Paul contemplated the negative side, so to speak, of Christianity. His inspired pen has described with surpassing clearness the motions of sin. None who study his writings can have light views of the wickedness of any manifestation of it. Evil propensities, worldly desires, resentments, self-will, and all forms of selfishness, are by him so represented that no Christian can under his treatment judge himself leniently in these things. But oh, the unspeakable comfort of the Pauline views to those who are in earnest to be delivered from this life of sin. There may be such delightful consciousness of deliverance from guilt, such sweet sense of being no more a prodigal child, an orphaned creature; there may be such mastery obtained over passions, such destruction of evil tempers, such crucifying of self, all this and more, implied in death to sin, even in this world, is distinctly contemplated by these words and elsewhere taught by Paul. The idea of the future destiny of the believer is that of the completest victory over evil. Sin is to have no existence in the soul; not a shadow of fear, not a root of bitterness is to remain in the regenerate self. And yet this is only a negative description of the Christian state. The verse is richer in positive meaning. For though to be dead to sin does imply life to holiness, this latter needs its independent prominence before we have the full meaning of Christianity. This we have when the Apostle adds "And your life is hid with Christ in God. You live now, morally live, you are alive unto God! A new divine life exists in you, such as constitutes the moral condition and character of unfallen beings, such as men ideally true must be conceived to be, such as the normal original man was. That life is one of restored creatureship and sonship to God. Your dependence is an easy, grateful relation. You love now to live, move, and have your being in God. It is your great glory to leave all things in his hands. You have no terror concerning him, therefore you fear nothing else. You find exalted pleasure in offering him the sacrifice of a creature, and gratefully adore him as your glorious Creator. Your filial relation is one of dignity, and love, and joy. You feel what immense honor it is that you should be called sons of God! Your heart fills with humble confidence as you exercise the spirit of adoption and cry Abba, Father. It is to you unspeakable enjoyment, that as a child you have access to the Infinite Father, and feel assured that he hears and graciously answers your prayers, and in all things watches over you." So then this life is the favor of God felt in the soul and thrilling in human consciousness. But it is yet more, it is indwelling holiness; it is a nature of goodness; it is love to God; honor to him; submission to him; acceptance of his will even in trials; cheerful obedience to him in all things; and a constant seeking for his glory as the end of human existence. It is love to man, a love which embraces all, independent of natural affection, which seeks the good of all, which is tolerant of all, which bears the burdens of all, feeling good will to them irrespective of conduct, blessing them, no matter what they say, and do, and are. This life is the fruit of a holy nature; it is a life of humility, and meekness, and gentleness; it is spontaneous, a stream from a fountain. In its newly arranged order, conscience is supreme over intellect, and natural affections, and appetites, and senses; while these, duly cultivated, are imbued with benevolence. Neither death to sin nor life to holiness is complete here, but, considered in respect to the certainty of its entire possession of the soul, at last, this life is viewed now as actually thus complete. It is often very sad to be taught that it is indeed far enough from triumphing over every present agency of sin. Even where it really exists, trial too frequently discovers its imperfect mastery of the character, and this is why so few rise above the measure of average goodness. It is the great grief of true Christians to find in themselves so little of divine life and to see so much and suspect more that is not imbued by it. Still wherever it exists it is sure finally to engross the whole soul, and even in this world there is immense encouragement to earnest hearts in the revelation we are studying. Paul is inspired to give you ennobling views of what a man may acquire of holiness in this life. Indeed this is just the peculiarity of these doctrines which have a side so massive with guilt and sin—that they have also another side correspondingly bright with joy and genial with goodness! Yes, you may attain wondrous peace and surprising fruits of heavenly culture. But this is more evident when we enter into the final conception of this "life as hid with Christ in God." "We have a mediator between God and man!" is the full statement of our glorious faith. Jesus Christ exhausts every idea of mediation. He unites in himself the divine and human, strangely separated by the great original shock, working on before our eyes. The very completeness of humanity in which he hath manifested himself on the side towards us, presents our nature in its entire excellence, and is made the palpable means of our redemption. He is to us this eternal life in every sense. In him we have redemption, the forgiveness of sins. United to him, his righteousness *is ours*. Into all that willing, loving sacrifice we enter, and what we instinctively try to make for ourselves, "expiation," but cannot—no, never—is nevertheless ours in him. Yes, our propitiation is made in him. He is our propitiation. With no presumption, yet with an awful and thrilling sense of identity, adoring humbly, yet confidently, the Christian feels in his union to Christ every part of reconciliation with God and the moral universe, effected. This is a life of restored creatureship and sonship in and with Christ. Again in him we have redemption, even now, and creation into his image. We are made partakers of his nature and bear the fruits of the Spirit, freely given in him. We are united to him, as the branch of the vine to its vigorous stock. This is his own sweet illustration. The fruits of that vine, the characteristics of true heavenly manhood, come out in beauty and grow and ripen as he prunes and cultivates. Yes, all that is great and good in Christian life, all humble, gentle, lowly tempers, all strong, healthy conscience, all subordinated senses, and intellect, all love to God, all consecration of self to him, all good will to men, all heroic endurance and generous doing and magnanimous sentiments, and kindly feelings, manifest themselves out from this life with Christ, and are its free impulses as it is itself quickened and refreshed from Christ the life. The believer looks to his Lord as the sufficient source of all regenerate activity, as the foundation of all holy nature in himself. Not as to a rite or theological formula, not as to an order of devotions and rule of conduct only, but as to a living person overflowing with life, does he turn to his Redeemer. As he feels and fears his unity with his race, whose vitality of evil, extending in nations and families, sends degenerate life through him, so he feels and loves his unity with his Lord, in himself a new and holy humanity, whose affluence of good ever communicates grace to him. To him that blessed person is distinct and full reality, in whom he lives, as when in moments of highest, dearest Christian consciousness he says, "I live, yet not I but Christ liveth in me, and the life which I now live in the flesh I live by the faith of the Son of God, who loved me and gave himself for me." But this is not the whole. As Christ is hid in God, so is the believer's life which is with Christ. The very completeness of divinity, which has been manifested by the Eternal Son, presents on the side towards God, the fullness of the Godhead, the divine nature in its Infinite personality. In Christ this is clearly revealed as the ground of our redemption. If, in the original creation, he is the creator, as when it is said "All things were made by him and without him was nothing made that was made," equally is the Son the author of the new creation. The manifestation of himself in our nature, at once the climax of all conceivable relations and that most adapted to our wants, conducts us to God himself. It is plain from the harmonious intimations of all preceding revelations, and Christ's oft repeated declaration, that it is the divine intention that with reverence, yet with nearness, we should gaze, as in light chastened to our mortal vision, upon God. Oh, how can we fail to perceive this is the great substance of our Saviour's mediation, and that he would have us feel that our God is thus made known to us, so near in all majesty and power, and so attractive in love. Yes it is our sublime faith that Christ was hid in God, that he who took upon him our nature, and whom the eye saw, and the ear heard, and the hand touched, was " in the beginning with God and was God!" But if our life be with Christ, then is it hid with him in God. It is hid in him, certainly, as concerns all contrast with seeming outward evils. The Apostle frequently turns the minds of Christians away from what they appeared to the world, which looked through a medium discolored by sin, and rated character and condition by glare and sensual advantage, to their real estimation with God. How often he bids them remember that though despised and persecuted with men, they were honorable and safe with God. The outward was only the delusion of an hour, a spell of false vision cast by the magic of evil, and devilish malice. It would not last always. Meanwhile the exulting consciousness was theirs of being God's own children, " heirs of God and joint heirs with Christ to an inheritance incorruptible and full of glory." But this is not all the meaning of a life hid with Christ in God, else it were making a platitude of one of the most profoundly rich truths of Christianity. It is hid in the deeper sense of having its root and ground in the Divine Being! the soul of man estranged from God is restored in Christ. All that is included in the mystery of our separation from the Father of our spirits, illustrates the extent of our reunion to him. As the rude convulsion of our fall has uptorn our moral nature from its once glorious basis so now this life hid with Christ in God is the reëstablishing of our moral nature in its original home. The believer may well rejoice in his union to Christ; for united to Christ his soul resumes its true place, and is reunited to its almighty source of spiritual life. In Paul's fullest statements of redemption, in John's delightful chapters on the Christian's sonship and his living union to God, you have this magnificent view of regenerate life. But perhaps nowhere is a believer's ground of life so impressively presented, as in our Lord's Intercessory Prayer. When one reads that wondrous prayer, and considers that it is our Lord's own sense of the relation of Christians to God, it is impossible not to be struck with the amazing destiny it opens to them. The circumstances in which he utters it, render it of as much moment to our full conception of Christ as his temptation, for if that assures us of his actual sympathy with us, as well as reveals the vast empire of evil in which we are living and which he has conquered, this equally assures us of our Saviour's actual intercession for us as united to him, and reveals that heavenly kingdom to which we belong, and whose divine sovereignty is his own. And then it is not discourse, but prayer. At other times Christ teaches us to pray. Here he prays himself. Prayer always presents the truth, we believe, most simply and naturally. But how impressive are the grand facts of redemption as seen in the softened reflection of Christ's prayer. As on some lake amid snow mountains, in a night of beauty never to be forgotten, one looks into calm depths and sees stars mirrored with luminous distinctness, so may we, as we read that chapter, reverently gaze down into the depths of Jesus' holy soul, and behold imaged there in forms of tenderest expression the truths of our Christian state. And oh! what conclusions we may, without presumption, draw of the glory that shall be revealed! But still deeper than this, and its assurance too, is the unmistakable revelation there, that the Christian's life is hid in God, that its ground is in God himself. Yes, we, if truly with Christ, once wild, degenerate, long isolated, self-centred souls, rooted too in this human unity of guilt and sin, are now returned with Christ into the glorious source of all moral good. Our life is hid in God, in him the Almighty Life, from whose fullness, all holy being proceeds. Oh, what a faith is this! How can we wonder that such a soul as Paul gloried in it, and that he could rise so independent of our low motives and excitements when these ideas mastered him, and this experience lighted up his consciousness. Is it strange that John, once so anxious for place for himself and brother, could become so superior to the lust of the eye, and the pride of life, when this gospel was his and this life pulsated within him? Oh, can any of us afford to do or be mean in our ambitions, and resentments and discontents when the lofty aims and resplendent future of such existence may be ours?

Think then, first, of the safety of this life with Christ. Nothing can pluck the believer out of the Almighty hand. This heavenly plant can never be rooted up. It is possible to tear from its soil the mightiest tree of earth, but he whose life with Christ is hid in God, can never be removed. This life may be assailed long and fiercely here, but it can never be torn away from its source. The new humanity can never fail, for its life begins in a divinely human head, and its hidden ground is deep in the almightiness of God. The believer may then fearlessly encounter trouble of poverty or far greater woes, may rest from fear of calamity, for he abideth in God. Death and hell are great enemies, but Christ has conquered death and hell. Yes, disciple, when doubts and weary questionings might darken your future, when you might look out into a starless night of ages and be oppressed with dreadful silence, you need no meteor image from out sick souls to comfort or assure you of immortality, but behold! on the horizon of time and of eternity, the glorious form of your Mediator. Up from your inmost soul rushes the consciousness "Because he lives I shall live." Think too, secondly, how the wants of man and the sufficiency of Christ reciprocally illustrate each other. If the personal revelation of Jesus Christ discovers us more thoroughly to ourselves, and in the light which he throws upon human condition and character, men's guilt and sinfulness become more apparent, so on the other hand do the most inward moral necessities of man made manifest in the course of human development refer themselves with amazing significancy to the corresponding sufficiency of help in Christianity. It has been deemed a great thing to produce individuality. This is one effect and cause of civilization. Nay, above all else the gospel directly and indirectly quickens and enlarges it. It separates men in condition and thought from the mass and makes them individual, so that slavery in mind or conscience becomes impossible. But here too man's sin acts in its inevitable tendency to pervert and exaggerate. So individuality becomes individualism, its monstrous caricature. Behold it in our day appearing in many forms, each of them characteristically evil and repellent to sound thinking and healthy feeling. See it in political history, where it makes shallow and unprincipled demagogues; in the religious world, where it makes ministers separate from their work and intensely self-conscious. See it in young men who, early severed from the sweet subordination of home, by the forced life of society, become reckless of restraint from those who love them, undesirous of culture, and with ill furnished intellect, weak affections, and low consciences, rush unprepared into the strife of men; self-satisfied even when they fail of true manhood. Remark it even in those women, the monstrous product of our civilization, who break away from the gentle unities of life, where real men love to yield to their intuition of reason, higher than our logic, and to their gentleness, mightier than our rudeness, and who, ceasing to be women, are still not men. See it all around us in pettiest men who, for lack of better, occupy position and decide questions of moment, who, not educated enough to feel their want of education, are perfectly content with themselves, and could have taught Solomon in the glory of his wisdom, and then have travelled complacently to Athens to settle questions for Plato. Nay, go higher and contemplate some really kingly intellect who has climbed an Alpine summit of thought, and there lost a personal God in huge abstraction of self, and merged all the tragic realities and affections of humanity in his own individualism. We think vice and passion dreadful, but a remorseless egoism may, in the sight of God be worse, and nearer the last capacity of evil. Long after we may have escaped the fangs of excess, and become decent with the amenities of life, nay, have made ourselves sincerely exact in religious forms and works, the unchanged soul may have withdrawn its strength of evil within, and there in a focus of unloving selfishness, may be burning with unholy self-consciousness, ready to thrill out in electric shocks of malevolence, when pride, or interest, or will is crossed.

Oh, what may individualism grow to be? Who can follow without shuddering, a self-conscious soul, with all its diseased sensitiveness, into eternity? The Bible representations, and particularly our Lord's parable of the Prodigal Son, treat the isolation of self, the centering of all in self, as the first manifest beginning of sin, as the inward source of outward transgression. Hence we need a more radical change than one which leaves the self unchanged in its final relation to God. We need something to meet that far within defect of which individualism is one of the expressions. So in every age have most thoughtful men felt that the greatest hindrance to growth in Christian life, was this exaggerated self-consciousness, this self-centralization. Man is indeed a soul lost out of the sweet attractions of a divine center, and wandering wild in cycles of guilt, and sin, and error. Now, the aspect of Christianity which we have been studying, "The Life hid with Christ in God," is that of restoration to original dependence and harmony. There is indeed no loss of normal individuality, but an individuality, enlarged and beautified, and full of intelligent life in love. There is no destruction, nor even lessening of personality. This indeed becomes more complete and alive with idea and feeling, more susceptible of fellowship with other persons, from God to the youngest Spirit. But it is entire deliverance from this morbid self, the repression of this swollen selfhood. It is repose of soul in harmony with God. It is final rest in an Almighty Father from the despotism of thought and the tyranny of nature.

And this I preach to-day! I preach it to you self-conceited and weary questioner. I preach it to you, religionist, selfishly sensitive, or hard with legal spirit, feebly appreciating the genial love of Christ. I preach it to you, struggling and chafing sufferer. To you, man of ambition or pleasure, toiling ever and ever dissatisfied. And to every soul conscious of an exaggerated and disquieted self.

Jesus Christ can cure the fever of the soul. As when on the earth, he laid his gentle hand on leprous wretches, so may he heal our inmost hurt.

Prodigals of earth return to the rest which remains. Seek "the life hid with Christ in God."

Preached at the Installation of
Rev. J. Lewis Diman, Brookline, 1860.

The Glorious Gospel of the Blessed God.

1st Timothy. 1. 11.   "According to the glorious gospel of the blessed God."

SUCH seemed the faith of Christ to Paul, and we would understand the views which drew from him this strong expression ; for he uttered it when the great and noble of earth were insensible to Christianity, and when he was preaching its unappreciated excellence, mid persecution, and contempt, and stupidity. The condition of human apprehension that makes the impression of an outward object dependent on the inward state of the observer, a condition often overlooked, but accounting for many changes of opinion, many surprising beliefs and theories, applies eminently to religious truth. In our probation the possibility of uncertainty is a necessary element, and it is reasonable to suppose that some of the evidences of God himself, and his providence, and his redemption, would depend very much on the state of the observer. Much more conceivable is it, that when received as true, they would seem very different to different persons. Thus, God might appear very terrible to an accusing conscience, while he would be an object of reverential delight to a holy heart. So the redemption by Christ might excite no feeling of adoration in a worldly, or coldly intellectual soul, when to a penitent, loving spirit, it might be " the glorious gospel of the blessed God." We do not look from Paul's great height of Christian vision. Ours is not his profound experience of spiritual life, and therefore we do not see in the same clearness of moral light the objects of his admiration. The medium through which we view redemption is dim, and so its glory is obscured. But we can at least contemplate some of the aspects in which the gospel is glorious. And

1. It is so in its origin. It is "the gospel of the blessed God." It proceeds from the Infinite Being who, possessed of boundless happiness himself, desires the blessedness of his creatures. "It is the power of God." Who can forgive sins but God? Who can morally renew fallen man, and restore him to his true relations, but his Almighty Creator? Its Saviour is the Son of God, manifest in miracles, and word of authority that comes from creative power. Its inspirations are not genius, nor philosophy, nor the progressive mind of the race; they are the teachings of the Holy Ghost! Its restraining, convicting, and regenerating influences are not rites, nor reform, nor mere argument: they are the action of that Holy Spirit within the soul of man. Its resources of life, whereby it bursts forth from decayed churches, with the freshness of its morning, are no reserved energy of opinion, but the characteristic of exhaustless power, such as belongs only to the God of this ever reviving creation.

So, secondly, is it the *wisdom* of God; this harmonious adaptedness to the utmost wants of man, exhausting his higher nature, and comprehending his lower, developing and filling his individual character, yet embracing his social history, and signifying the destiny of his race, is not human but divine wisdom. Its wondrous course through the ages, its triumphs, its overruled reverses, its fitness to every political and social condition, and noiseless transformation of these into final correspondence with itself, its mastery of human sin from the treason of Judas to the last act of wickedness, making it minister to purposes of good. All this is not the " councils of men," but the wisdom of the Eternal.

Thirdly, it is the love of God. It proceeds from infinite benevolence. Man is selfish; God is love. That forgiveness so immense, came not from the conclusions of the vindictive human heart, but from the boundless compassions of God. That love which loved us even while we were yet sinners, was no thought of gloomy, remorseful, misgiving man, but the revelation of infinite mercy. Its charity includes the race, and asserts the essential brotherhood of men in face of universal selfishness, entrenched in caste, maintained by state, sanctioned by society, and defended by philosophy. The gospel establishes this on a moral basis, which nothing can overturn, and which surely wins its way to human faith. Reciprocal virtues spring from this charity, morally superior to the partial and unloving qualities of human intercourse elsewhere taught. All this originated not with pent-up, self-loving, national, classified, and sectarian man, but with Him who so loved us, as to "give his Son to die for us."

Even in this twilight of low moral state, and limited experience, we can feel that the divine origin of the gospel is approved by its harmony with all else we may know of God and his works. It is in harmony with the noblest conception of himself formed in the human soul, with his creation without, its laws and their happy results and penalties, with his providence, as its great and minute events develop principles of moral government, and indicate the purposes and character of an infinite mind. It is in harmony with the soul itself, God's chiefest natural manifestation, with the moral sense's instinctive utterance of an eternal right, and with man's spiritual nature relating him to an immaterial world, and to immortality. It deals with society as a vaster humanity, whose logical completeness and perfect ideal, demand Christianity; as Christianity finds its fullest actuality only in regenerate society.

Such are the magnificent claims of the gospel. It demands our faith, not as the highest product of man, but as the salvation of God. Its course is not uncertain beginnings growing by mythical accretions, from human traditions into system, but the complete will of the Almighty conducted by his eternal purpose through no doubtful nor obscure dispensations, from its first dawning light, to the brightness of its personal revelation. Awful with consequences, it comes to us in the dignity of this divine origin. Full of God it presents itself to separated souls as the mediating creation of God. It asks no accommodating reception, as in part our work, but a childlike faith, as his redemption. The River of Life, it flows out from the Infinite Fountain, immediate and heavenly, *his* gospel, and therefore glorious, with the glory of God.

II. This gospel is glorious in itself. First, in its great person, the Lord Jesus Christ. Seen amid the ruins of earth, he stands alone in the glory of his humanity. It is the perfection of our nature, a mind of wondrous intuitions, a conscience of supreme power and perfect correspondence with the eternal right, a will of entire conformity to the Divine affections; of absolute purity. That holy Just One! So free from every sin of man, no defect marring His completeness, no fierce spirit ever flashing out, no ambitious tempers ever aspiring, no vain emotions ever contracting, no selfish purpose ever soiling, no feverish self-consciousness, but a life hid in God, and overflowing with love to Being. Lofty in virtue, but full of tenderest sympathy; untouched by evil, and separate from sinners, he was yet the friend of sinners.

Oh, his indeed, is the dignity of human nature! When we think of ourselves and others, there are times when it is hard to reverence this nature of ours. We are so degenerate! But when we regard Christ, and see our nature as it appears in him, then we gain exalted conceptions of what man were but for sin, and turn with respect to the lowest, and honor, even in its ruins, that which in Christ proves itself capable of such transcendent excellence.

III. This exalted personage is glorious in the glory of Divinity, which this perfect human nature enshrines. In it is manifested the Son of God. In that unruined temple dwells the Eternal Word, and out from it shines the glory of God. That power to control nature, its tempests, and diseases, and deaths, that authority over minds of men and spirits, that knowledge so perfect, that wisdom so profound, that forgiveness of sins, that sublime claim of heavenly fellowship, that unmistakable assertion of him whom we cannot doubt without disbelief in all truth and right, is God. It is He "who in the beginning was with God and was God." He who thus "took upon him our form" and was "made in the likeness of us sinful men, yet thought it no robbery to be equal with God." That glory which appears so resplendent in creation, and Providence, and inspiration, that which manifests itself in Christ, and here, in gracious accommodation to our wants, becomes more distinct as embodied in human personality. Now we have the climax of the revelation of God to man, and in Christ we behold the glory of God and adore with simple, intelligent faith. Oh, how chastened the splendors, and yet how near, the presence of God in such a manifestation! Since man is capable of the idea of God, and of receiving divine communication at all, whether through nature or inspiration, since man, when morally excited, in every age, uniformly "feels after, if haply he may find God," how is it possible to conceive of his being revealed to the human soul in a manner more suited to its constitution and worthier even of the Divine Being? The heart that delights in creation, and Providence, and inspiration, must rejoice in these mild glories so personal and so full in Christ.

But this gospel is glorious in itself, as respects the work of Christ. It is this indeed which chiefly concerns us sinful men. Christ has entered our world not merely to manifest God, for this alone might be terror to estranged and guilty creatures, nor merely to illustrate what man should be, for the exhibition of our original unfallen humanity in its perfect holiness, might, by its contrast with us actual men, convict us more utterly of guilt and overwhelm us with shame and hopelessness. The glorious work of Jesus Christ is redemption. He identifies himself with us, entirely fulfilling every condition of our existence, to save us from ruin. So he subjects himself to law, by virtue of his humanity. So he exposes himself to its penalty, and submits to death. "No one taking his life, himself having power to lay it down and power to take it again, he lays down his life for us." A willing sacrifice, he puts himself where are only sinners—he suffers as only sinners suffer. Thus he becomes sin for us, that by his unity with us, we "might become the righteousness of God in him." Our glorious head; the second Adam. We live in him and are accepted in him. "He gave himself a ransom for us." "He is the propitiation for our sins," the mediator between God and man. In his divinely human personality, he reconciles us to God by his endurance of our woe, and justifies us by his perfect righteousness imputed to us. In a world where continually is repeated and illustrated on largest and smallest scale, through good and evil, happiness and misery, the vicarious condition of human existence, his redemption is the climax of that condition, harmonizing and crowning it by his identifying himself with us. And this is the glory of his work of love. Oh how can any sensitive soul fail to apprehend the excellence of Christ's work? If the highest sublimity in things moral be when men cheerfully endure great woes and even death for others, surely this willing offering of himself by Christ is the very height of moral greatness. If purest beauty appear in sentiments and acts of self-denial, and we esteem them in proportion to the dignity and heartiness of the self denied, surely there is a beauty surpassingly desirable when such a self as Christ, obeying only the constraint of love, "bears our sins and carries our sorrows," and "redeems us by his precious blood." Even when slightly touching those analogies of which our system is full, yet still undoubtedly recognizing the universal principle they illustrate, the Apostle rises as if to an unapproachable summit in speaking of Christ. "For a good man one might even dare to die, but God commendeth his love to us, in that while we were yet sinners, Christ died for us."

Ah, it is because we are so low, morally, that love appears no more glorious. Yet we are ready to admit that it is the substance of morality. And we believe, too, that our moral nature is highest. Brute strength is not our excellency, else animals and machines were more excellent. Intellect is not our chief glory, else we must exalt devils. We court the rich, but we are ashamed of it. We honor statesmen and philosophers, but we have to conceal their vices, and prove them virtuous, else our conscience reproaches us. There is something in us, which claims our allegiance to goodness, and makes us feel that it is true grandeur of soul.

Now love, holy and disinterested, is the very bloom and heart of goodness. It is the soul of human virtue. It is the infinite worthiness of God. It is the dignity of angels, and fills heaven with light and happiness. It is the greatness of man restored to his original excellence, and its deeds and affections glance brightness across the gloom, and break the monotony of human selfishness. But Christ's work of redemption is the unequalled act of love. His cross gathers around it all the capacity of benevolence. Here meet and center all rays of vicarious good will. His is a sacrifice, in perfect intelligence and willingness, of sinless purity, of sympathy perfected into identity with the guilty.

You and me, in our godless, dark state of sin, so loved that Christ died to save us! Are we not high enough in moral sensibility to enter somewhat into the feelings of the Apostle and see the glory of the gospel in itself? Can we not appreciate something of the admiration which the visions of the Apocalypse breathe when the love of Christ is the object of thought and song? Do we not recognize some reflections of this love on earth in the most ennobling actions of men who have been moved by their experience of its benefits to labor for their fellow creatures?

Are we so sunk in material pursuits and intellectual tastes, that we cannot understand the ideas and emotions of the highest moral natures in every age, the holiest and noblest spirits who have found in the cross of Christ a glory which transcended all human conceptions? Oh, come not to its contemplation as to a scene in creation, a piece of art, a poem or an argument, with sensual nature predominant, or intellect cultivated at the expense of conscience. Look not on the work of Christ as one who has no interest in it, with superficial consciences, the deepest wants of the soul unfelt, a partial, untrue man, stupidly self-complacent, because having no high standard of manhood, a guilty sinner who ignores his guilt and will not see his sin, esteeming wealth, or honor, or pleasure, or knowledge, or talent above goodness, the world above God, and time above eternity. But come to it as an object of vastest moral concern. Look on the work of Christ, as one who has immortal interests in it, with the whole feelings of an actual man true to yourself, conscious of deepest wants, as a sinner, feeling yourself such, in view of the real standard of human character, valuing moral excellence above every thing else. Come with a conscience fully alive, come humble, penitent, and then see if the redeeming work of Christ will not seem glorious in a sinner's eyes.

IV. Finally, the gospel is glorious in its ends. These are the noblest that we can conceive of, the honor of God, the salvation of men. First, the great object in all creation is to glorify the Creator. Thus do "the heavens declare the glory of God." Man's own conscience approves the fundamental obligation that whatsoever a moral creature does, he should "do all to the glory of God." Man's own convictions confirm the statement of his sins, as made by revelation, that "he has come short of the glory of God," and that men are without excuse "because when they knew God they glorified him not as God." So man should see in nature, and be led by science, to recognize an infinite mind, and come through all art, and philosophy, and history to sublime conclusions of Providence. So should the study of his own wondrous constitution of soul fill him with impressions of its glorious maker, who thus manifests himself in a creation so marvellous as a human soul.

Now the gospel glorifies God in different aspects. First, it vindicates his eternal justice. This is the basis and essential stability of moral character and government. Sometimes men speak as if God made the moral laws which govern us, and established by his arbitrary will, alone the fixedness of right. But a moment's thought might convince anyone that a right fixed by the arbitrary will, even of God, could not be essential right. The instinctive action of our own conscience assures us of the inherent distinctions of morality. We find in ourselves the certainty of justice being vindicated. We vindicate it upon ourselves as far as our cognizance of the moral relations involved extends. There is no choice left us. If our moral sense be alive, the same sensibility which approves good, and the happy consequences that follow the good, acts with equal spontaneousness in reproving the evil, and affirming the unhappy consequences that follow the evil. The conscience thus takes for granted a absolute law, and its instinctive decisions manifest to us such law as existing in the nature of things. With this agrees perfectly the manner in which revelation presents the law. The vindication of right is there declared to be equally concerned in blessings and in penalties. The necessity of this discrimination is there treated as an ultimate fact in the universe, as something inherent in the government of God, as characteristic of his nature whereby he is holy, and not as anything created by him. To satisfy then even the living human conscience, to honor the essential idea of right, much more to glorify God who is the infinite impersonation of right, law must be vindicated. Preëminently does the gospel accomplish this. Jesus Christ made clear the glory of the law by his teachings, still more by his life, and most of all by his sufferings and death. On the side of its observance we behold him magnifying it, as earth has not seen before. On the side of its violation, we see him, in his work of saving its violators, not lowering it, not putting away its necessary penalty, but in his identity with us enduring that penalty. Oh what impressions of eternal right does the soul gather at the cross of Christ! If suffering, encountered willingly in behalf of others, establishes our conviction of the stability of natural law, much more does the love of Christ, submitting to a vicarious death, illustrate the immovable foundations of moral law, and destroy all delusion of impunity to sin.

Again, the gospel glorifies God in manifesting his mercy. Nature interpreted by the misgiving human soul, speaks doubtingly of pardon. Revelation declares it with ever increasing clearness. "The Lord our God plenteous in mercy," is its cheering strain. Old prophets loftily uttered it, the Psalmist sweetly sang it, and sacred historians recorded it. But the gospel is the very fullness and distinctness of the declaration of God's mercy. There indeed God shines out in the radiance of his forgiving love. In the person and work of Jesus Christ, we guilty men have the highest assurance that our God will be merciful to us. The gospel, in this respect is as if an arch of magnificent hope were spanning earth, while all above and around, clouds of gloomy judgments are breaking, and their thunders dying away. But, secondly, it most concerns us, that it is a glorious end of the gospel, to save man. This it does in the fullest sense. It saves him from the condemnation of sin. "To him that is in Christ Jesus, there is henceforth no condemnation." In Christ, man is fully pardoned. By him he comes to God, as his creature accepted and rejoicing with joyful reverence, as a child returned to his father and restored to favor. Adopted in Christ, his is no more the spirit of bondage, full of fears and serving as a slave of unsatisfying forms, but the spirit of adoption, full of filial confidence, gladly obeying with a free will. United to Christ, he is a joint heir with Christ to a splendid inheritance. His soul is elastic with hopes and expectations. He is raised from degradation to original dignity of manhood. Nay, he is made a King and Priest unto God. Oh, what a future of nobleness for this world even, and much more in the next, opens to man in the gospel! What new and exalted anticipations it warrants! The earth wears another aspect, and human history lights up with resplendent destiny.

Again, the gospel saves from the pollution of sin. It makes man "a new creature in Christ." He is "born of the Spirit," and bears the "fruits of the Spirit." Become a branch of the heavenly vine of humanity, he derives hence a holy life. As he has borne the image of the first Adam, so he hath impressed on him the image of the second. In him "is crucified the old man with his lusts, and he puts on the new man with his affections." The old things of insubordinate propensities, of ambition, and avarice, and all selfishness, of alienation from God, and discord with man, pass away and all things become new, new characters, new relations, new purposes, new desires. He loves God and his fellows, exercises holy affections, seeks the honor of God and good of men, is adorned with gentle virtues, and prepared for exigencies, fitted for the enjoyments and harmonies of heaven. Thus the gospel saves man! Its end is to restore him fully, to produce a new creation. It designs to replace these ruin of humanity, by the structure of a city of God, a Kingdom of heaven composed of regenerated men. Surely this is to us, a glorious end. By these and other views, we may understand that the revelation of Christ is, indeed, the "glorious gospel of the blessed God."

Surely then it is a great thing to apprehend, and partake, and proclaim this glory. Angels sang exalted praises of it, and in sublime summary comprehended its blessedness. "Glory to God in the highest, peace on earth, and good will to man." Happy spirits in heaven honor it in glowing strains "Worthy is the Lamb that was slain to receive riches, and wisdom, and strength, and honor, and glory, and blessing." What wonder that Paul gloried in the cross of Christ, and esteemed all things but loss, in such comparison. Its thought mastered his intellect, and its spirit possessed his soul. By its reflection on his character he was ennobled, and its impulses constrained him to heroic love,—lifting him quite above other men. The same gospel remains, with divine truth, and energy unexhausted. We have referred to the sad subjective power in us to contract, and deform, and fossilize everything without us, the gospel thus often ceases to be glorious in our administration of it, when we utter its inspirations as dead dogmas. But this concerns not the magnificent capacities inherent in redemption. To what height may its ideas elevate above crude notions, and partial views, and meteor reforms! What superiority to worldly passions and agitations is possible! What emancipation from formalism, and mere ecstasies! What vigor of holy life may engross the soul! To what untiring benevolence may men be lifted above all gross and refined selfishness, and how may feverish self-consciousness disappear in the love of Christ! What moral stability, and independence, are attainable for lives hid with Christ in God! And who shall limit the conception of character that may be formed out of truth—so massive with force, so replete with tenderness, whose contrasts of supernatural grace are made more luminous, by the sombre sides of condemning nature. So from hearts full of living apprehensions may men come to speak with authority and win attention, and compel assent to words as significant and fresh, as when Paul uttered them ages since. If only the minister, in our days, can lose himself in this great theme and receive indeed baptism of the Holy Ghost into the life of this gospel, he will need seek no supplement to Christianity, no fire from strange shrines to keep alive the flame on his own altar. A Christian pastor, he shall find in the unexaggerated exercise of that office, enough to occupy all his powers and subordinate to its duties, all culture, every manly virtue and quality, and fine taste, all emotions from indignation at moral wrong to mirthfulness, all natural affections and human sympathies, he will need them all, and the largest and most genuine of them in his function. He will not have to curtail any of the man in him to suit his pastorate, nor go elsewhere for scope to think, and feel, and act. Conflict—deep thought—lofty imaginings—quiet purpose—there is room for all in the real pastor's life. There is no spirit of self-sacrifice too costly to be used in his unostentatious history, no sensibility too precious to be wasted in his daily relations, and no benevolence too expansive for parish emergencies. When in our day the alternative often seems stagnation in actual life, or activity in theatric existence, only the gospel's full possession of the soul can keep it alive and graceful in ungazetted duties. Then, indeed, the ideal may approach to reality, and what our restless country needs for its homes and churches may come to be a wholesome fact. Pastors who, with healthy brain and growing intellect, and quick conscience, and loving, genial heart, preach "the glorious gospel of the blessed God."

So for the Pastor. But equally for all Christians were it a great thing to believe fully as a doctrine—feel strongly as an experience—contemplate habitually as an object—seek supremely as an end—and obey loyally as a motive—this glorious gospel. What a transformation would take place in our whole being if we could only rise to such views of our grand faith as Paul had. How different every thing would look in this world! What change in our estimates! How unlike the comparisons we now make! By what new tests we should try all in our existence! How worthless much that we now seek so eagerly! What restraints upon us! Could we fail to feel the ennobling influence of a vivid apprehension of such a faith? And then what transference of our best energies to highest aims! What repose of soul would be ours! Then to think of the rules of conduct which should govern us and the motives moving us! All this so vastly superior to what we think, and feel, and do now! For our religion is so above us. The glorious gospel we profess to believe, and which, in our slight way, we actually try to extend in the world, is so far exalted beyond our idea and practice of it! The world is full of instances of unappreciated privileges and opportunities. We are constantly seeing men living below their ideals. But what are these to our feeble participation in the splendid faith we call ours? Never till we see and feel more nearly as Paul did, how glorious is this gospel, shall we break the monotony of our selfish lives and be lifted out of our low average of conduct and character. Oh, believers in the glorious gospel, yes glorious though dimly seen, are you contented with your views? Can you read of self-denying faith and love aiming to live in the very place of others, and then keep on in the beaten track of a worldly Christianity? Surely there are times, even though long years have accustomed your life to run in these iron ruts of society, when you catch glimpses of the grandeur of your faith, and have nobler aspirations. Do you not long to be truly better men and to live nearer to the idea of this gospel? Oh, look more earnestly! Cherish those aspirations, for indeed, only profounder convictions than are common and a heartier appreciation of Christianity, can enable men to meet the exigencies of these times.

How strange that to any the gospel of the Son of God should be other than glorious! That they can see beauty in nature and art, yet no beauty in Christ, that they should desire him. What must we men be to prefer gain, or honor, or place, or letters, and turn away from the Saviour and his works? How wonderful that any awakened to some faint perception of their moral necessities, and the worth of Christ, can hesitate what course to pursue. For it remains true, assured by the word of God, and proved by myriads in every age, that the glory of the gospel waits to be manifested to all who seek its vision and experience. Yes upon eyes blinded with all this glitter of society, shall rise the majesty and loveliness of Christ. Into souls where now low values reign, thoughts full of market prices and social strifes for position, and gratifications, of self-conceit in superficial culture, feelings full of unworthy aims and ignoble motives, there shall come high estimates of divinest things, thoughts of noblest import, feelings of loftiest, purest tenor.

Oh, come in penitence bowing low; come in humble dependence! Ask earnestly, and you shall find how glorious is "the Gospel of the Blessed God."

The Grace of our Lord Jesus Christ.

(*Delivered August 13th, 1865.*)

II Corinthians, viii. 9. "For ye know the grace of our Lord Jesus Christ, that though he was rich, yet for your sake he became poor that ye through his poverty might be rich."

THE manner of Paul in this address to the Corinthian Christians, shows what he regarded as the great object of Christian faith, and the distinctive matter of Christian consciousness. So it supposes on their part an equally clear understanding of the same. "The grace of our Lord Jesus Christ." The purely undeserved, spontaneous love of Christ, of him who is Lord, absolute in dignity and power, their Lord upon whom they had no claim, and yet who, in his sovereign love, had done so much for them. It was this to which he referred them when he urged a particular duty as something of simplest truth. Notice now the way in which this grace manifested itself. And first, call to mind the state of our Lord before he appeared on earth to accomplish his work of love. The fullest recognition of this was necessary to the Apostle's argument. For men to feel the greatness of the sacrifice which they were to contemplate, they needed to recall the blessedness of the person making it. So it reads, "Though he were rich." Certainly not on earth, and those to whom Paul wrote, required not to be told where our Lord was rich, and in what respect. It was in previous and higher existence. That he existed before his appearance in human nature, was the simple faith of the church. Our Lord taught so plainly that he came from God and went to God, and that before Abraham was he is, it were strange if his disciples could have any other idea, and the constant tenor of Paul's preaching is to this effect throughout. Those men then, believed in a Being who had entered into their world from above. They thought of him as entirely apart from themselves and other men in this respect. But that was not all. They believed him to have been possessed of surpassing worth. He was rich in a divine personality. In the beginning with God and God himself. The glory which he had with the Father, was before the world. The blessedness he had enjoyed, was the eternal and unspeakable happiness of the only begotten Son in the bosom of the Father, a communion of which we may not think with presumptuous speculations, yet we may contemplate it with reverential delight. The power which he had, was that by which he created the world, so that "without him nothing was made that was made." The wisdom which he exercised, was that "which the Lord possessed in the beginning of his way, before his works of old, and which was set up from everlasting, and from the beginning, or ever the world was." The holiness which he possessed was that which abhorred evil and delighted in good, whose righteousness was eternal, and its justice such as could not clear the guilty, and its mercy plenteous towards the children of men. So was the love of our divine Lord everlasting, even from the foundation of the world, and such as no created thing could overcome! Thus was our Lord rich, before he took upon him our form. The riches of eternal power, and majesty, and truth, and holiness, and love were his! His, the wealth of heaven! In him the fullness of the Godhead! This was the Lord of whom Paul spoke to those Corinthians. This divine greatness, he must set before their minds, ere he reminds them of what their Lord did for them. This is our Lord, and we must simply and profoundly conceive of his divine Being and state, when we would have our hearts moved by the thoughts of what he hath done for us! Oh, think first always, of Jesus Christ as indeed our Lord; all power his, on earth and in heaven; glorious forever! No mere dogma, this, for belief, but a substantial reality for living faith to apprehend; a sufficient ground of truth for the mind to rest upon; a worthy object of reverence, and trust, and love for the heart to expend its whole capacity of affection upon. Then with this conception of what our Lord was, think, secondly, that for the sake of us sinful men he became "poor." Here, indeed, we are left in no obscurity, for the manifestation of Christ in our nature, his actual history on earth, was as luminous as the sun in heaven. It cannot be mistaken. How poor he became we can see ourselves. Poor in the very incarnation. However excellent in itself was the humanity which he took upon him, yet surely it was poverty beyond any comparison, for the infinite riches of heaven to be united with finite manhood, for all the fullness of Godhead to enshrine itself in human personality. If this manifestation went no farther, yet what goodness displayed! What condescension in this! What humbling, to use scriptural language, what "emptying of himself!" Surely this ought to awaken in our hearts deepest adoration and love. This should overawe our souls and strengthen our faith. This might abase us and excite us to an unreserved benevolence, if that were all the design of such a personal revelation. But this was not all. Our Lord became poor, in assuming all the conditions of our humanity.

We are sinners, and justly subject to the penalty of a violated law. We are treated in great measure as sinners; we are liable in greater measure. So Revelation expressly declares; so every man's conscience when awakened clearly affirms; so nature intimates. Now our Lord, in his divinely human person, subjected himself to penalty. We see that "he became a curse under the law." He came not as one who might justly be free from evils in our system, first in virtue of his sinless humanity, and surely by his divine power; but he came fully into our system, he partook of our very unity. It was no splendid figurative representation. He was made in all points like sinful men, except sin. He came not even as highest sinful man; not powerful, nor rich in state, but he was actually poor. Our Lord was poor. "He had not where to lay his head." No angels are poor, and I have yet to learn that there would be any poor saints on earth, if they were not sinners. Poverty is one of the consequences of violated law, and in this our Lord was identified with sinners. So also all through that wondrous life, so open to our view, he suffered as sinners suffer, and while all care seems taken to show that our Lord was tempted in all points as we are, and yet without sin, equal effort is made to impress us with his sharing the evils incident to a sinful and condemned race. We ought to dwell upon this, before we come to his death, for though that is rightly exalted, yet it is in virtue of its comprehending and crowning all his other sufferings. It is, indeed, a sublime whole that we should contemplate in our Lord's history, but if we do single out any suffering, it is as really an instance of his becoming a curse under the law, as was the final and extreme woe of death. But the poverty which our Lord took upon himself, is most fully shown in the penalty which he endured in his death. In this was most apparent, his power of immunity. "No man taketh my life. I have power to lay it down, and power to take it again," is his own distinct utterance in view of approaching death, and, mark that, he exhausts the penalty of death. Any death for him, must have been the "becoming poor of him who was rich," must have been the completion of his identifying himself with sinners. But to make this more entire; so to speak, to become, in this regard, most truly poor, he dies, not merely as all sinners die, but as sinners of sinners, as those condemned by solemn judicial process. Oh, there is immense significance in this. The crucifying of our Lord by the ecclesiastical authorities of the Jewish nation, and through the hands of the Roman civil power, is the most impressive and exhaustive fulfilling of this, "becoming poor." And if in all parts of our Lord's humiliation, it is plainly the divine intent, that we should behold him with unmistakable distinctness, this purpose is most fully accomplished in his death; for the circumstances connected with that event, are brought before the mind in such a light, that we seem to see it all as if passing in our very presence. We behold his sufferings in the garden, and hear his cries of mysterious agony. Surely his was poverty then, when not one of his disciples could enter into that awful loneliness, full of woe unknown to them. And had he not become poor indeed, when, deserted by all, he stood alone in Pilate's hall and endured that wicked rejection, that pitiless sentence, and those cruel mockings and scourgings? For that glorious Being to meet the deliberate denial of his Messianic dignity by the representatives of Judaism and Paganism, was the formal declaration of human society against him. Israel refused to receive its King and Saviour; the world refused its Redeemer; and when all this culminated in a judicial and ignominious death, and our Lord " was set forth, so evidently crucified, among men," what lower depth of poverty can we conceive of as being reached? Oh think what "becoming poor" was, when Christ submitted to such final penalty of the law! When he, possessed of unbounded resources, humbled himself to such depths of destitution. He, so rich in blessedness, permitted himself to be so filled with inconceivable wretchedness, and he, whose consciousness of unlimited power remained and gleamed out from his latent glory, subjected himself to unresisting impotency! Draw nearer and contemplate. It is meant we should think who it was that suffered on that cross. Then behold that crucifixion amid the powerlessness of those who loved him, and the triumphant malice of those who hated him! Then hear that strange cry which betokened a horror of darkness in the soul, an abyss of suffering, deeper than which our imagination cannot go, and we may have some idea of what is meant by our Lord Jesus Christ "becoming poor." The poverty of Christ in this full meaning! What a thought for us to dwell upon! When we think of men being poor in any thing and to any extent, it is nothing strange! Why should we not be poor in all respects? We are sinners and do not deserve any thing else. If we reflected deeply on our relation to God and his moral government, we should not wonder nor complain at any poverty. But when we consider the Lord Jesus Christ, his divinely human majesty and excellence, surely it were natural to associate with him all riches of possession, and state, and power. Ah, how many feel that they would eagerly give all these to him! Even those of us, who, with strange inconsistency, withhold so much of the same things from those, who he has told us, represent him, feel thus towards him; and we know that now in heaven, he is rich in glory. And yet "he became poor." His whole life in this world was nothing else. Dwell upon this, you his disciples who have earthly state, and power, and wealth. Your Lord had nothing of this. He was poor in all things. Think of this, you who have not sought him at all, whose whole heart is set upon this world, and who have gained much of it, the Saviour you must at last seek, was despised and rejected of men! Yes let all remember this; the Lord Jesus Christ, whom we profess to honor, manifested himself not merely in our human nature, which, even though he had assumed its most exalted state, was becoming poor, but in that nature as least honored by earthly prosperity, and most characterized by suffering. It is intended we never should forget this. But, on the contrary, always bear in mind that our divine Lord lived on this earth, not as we, but poor in every sense, a man of sorrows and acquainted with grief. Yes, thus took on him the Blessed One, and then consider, thirdly, that he became poor for our sakes; surely it ought to need no argument that the humiliation of such a Being, so utter, and yet so willing, must have been vicarious on account of others, we are left in no possible doubt. It was that " through his poverty we might be rich." Through his poverty, on account of his humbling himself, and suffering. Thus he honored the law in all aspects. Thus he made propitiation for our sins. Repenting, acknowledging our utter poverty of soul. Receiving him by simple faith, we are united to him in an union as real as that which binds us to our race. We thus become identified with him as truly as he with us. In that precious union, we become rich, in every sense of our need. Rich in imputed righteousness, we are accepted in Christ freely and fully. "There is no condemnation to them in Christ." These are the assuring words, Christ is ours, and what his divinely human nature is, and has accomplished, we may without presumption appropriate as ours. Oh if there be a divine manifestation to save us, if indeed there be a Christ, what more palpable, nay, what more exhaustive way than this of identifying our Redeemer with us. Especially when so much of our evil came originally and so much comes every day, and must come on largest and smallest scale in the same way! Yes, here may be our confidence, we may live in the very light of the law, and we may have access unrebuked to the heavenly throne. For we are rich in the riches of Christ. He presents us! We will not fear since he is our advocate! Oh, who can exaggerate the riches of justification in Christ! What access, what humble trust for all future time! This for you, fearful disciple! Why torment yourself with examinations, impossible to satisfy! Why increase the burden of religious doings and turn the gospel into a bondage. Hear your Lord as he says, "Come unto me all ye that labor and are heavy laden and I will give you rest." In Christ is the very spirit of adoption; and this, too, is for any burdened soul. There cannot be a poverty felt so extreme that the riches of Christ's grace are not sufficient for it. Again we may be rich in inherent righteousness; united to Christ we may be made partakers of his holy nature; with Christ we receive the influences of the Spirit and are made new creatures in him, and then as from a new and living source, shall the fruits of a Christlike humanity make their appearance in our character. A morality of root, and branch, and luxuriant bearing. We may possess the virtues which in

Christ were so commanding and beautiful. The humility, the gracious tempers, the comprehensive love, may be ours. In these sinful hearts of ours may begin a work of good, a divine life of holiness which, even here under the culture of the Master's hand, may attain great excellence. What is there to forbid the highest aspirations after this likeness to Christ? The fullness of grace in him can never be exhausted; we can never offend him by importunity in asking for the blessing of holiness. It is we who limit these riches of our Lord! Nay, the world where we think it so hard to exercise the affections and virtues of Christianity, is the very world where the Saviour's own life was perfected, and where he established that kingdom in which his disciples may grow in the knowledge of him. Nay, in every age how have men attained to wondrous participation in these riches of Christ. Oh why do so many content themselves with such slight measures of Christian life, when they might be so rich in it! Why do any fail of it altogether, when they might partake of this priceless treasure! And, once more we may be made rich in the glory of Christ. United to him man becomes an heir with him to an inheritance glorious beyond thought. Our Lord has promised this himself. His high priestly prayer, so full of highest truth, encourages the loftiest expectation of glory when we enter upon the consummation of our redemption. Yes, man, once a noble creature, but now degenerate through sin, and at his best estate degraded, may, without presumption, look forward to transcendent glories. Such are some of the riches with which our Lord Jesus Christ enriches the children of men. What are all earthly possessions to them? What are the utmost treasures of this world without them? Poor, poor indeed are we if Christ makes us not rich. But rich enough if

Christ has given us these true riches, rich here, rich forever. And all this secured through the inconceivable poverty of our Lord Jesus Christ. He gave himself, the sacrifice beyond all price, that we might be blessed! Then we can understand something of the divine method of affecting the human heart. It is by presenting the grace of Christ. Thus it is employed here by Paul to excite in the Corinthian Christians, the spirit of benevolence towards the poor. It is unnecessary to dwell upon the prominence given to this charity in the early church, receiving from the Mosaic Institutes, the divine command on the care of the destitute. Still more instructed by the word and example of their divine Lord, the primitive disciples, living in communities full of poverty, and necessarily having many poor among themselves, were, from the first, trained to great responsibility in this matter. The church was understood to have a peculiar office in this regard. This work involved giving, on a scale which we have fallen off from, as we have from that of original missionary enterprise. The necessity of self-denial was then imperative. Hence, the test of liberality was sacrifice. And the question must have been, not what men gave, but what they had left. Read Paul's remarkable addresses to the churches, and we form an idea of the place this work held in the original conception of Christianity! To bring the conscience of men up to an obligation so imperative, to move them to such sacrifices as were demanded, is the apostle's aim. He stops at no lesser consideration, but points them at once to the sacrifice of Christ as the true measure of giving. He means just what he says. They were to be in the world as their Lord was. They were to give as he gave. It was to be sacrifice and if they felt their unity with their Lord, they would not withhold what was

Why are not the causes of some revolution to take place many hundred years hence, at work now? Why may they not have been at work ages back, before the flood? We cannot trace them thoroughly, but even we, the deeper we go, can see enough of this continuousness to confirm our conclusion from the nature of things. But he who created, and necessarily provided, must see these relations of history. Doubtless he who beholds the utmost vastness, must see also the extremest minuteness, of events. In this sense then, God beholds things more fully individual than we do, and one day with its incidents too slight to be noticed by us, is regarded by him with the same particularity as the drop of water with its insect world, where our microscopes cannot reach. But then his infinite knowledge embraces all these individual days with their minutest histories in a unity of time so absolute, that all ages are harmonized into one simple view. So the day expands beautifully, in that Almighty vision, into ages and the ages are gloriously comprehended in a day. With him, then, never so many years make any difference in the mysterious action of causes. He who of direct consequence arranged all, sees all in unbroken connection, and with him extent of time is of little account.

I. Let us illustrate this teaching from the Bible. One of God's titles, "Ancient of Days," expresses his comprehension of time. We think of some of our race who have lived very long, and years in their life seem far less of moment than in ours. But what is patriarchial life to that one thought, "Ancient of Days." In an immense past from which we recoil, our measures of time lessen in value to us. The sands increasing millions on the shore. The stars, numbering worlds on worlds, till even great suns cease to shine in single radiance, and we gaze on almost embodied masses of brightness. What are these to years in the idea of "Ancient of Days!" True not the least divisible moment is lost, but the number is infinite.

The whole scripture is full of simple, vast conceptions of the years of God. Nowhere is there any indistinct notion, never are these periods lost, but always for us, God is shown from everlasting years to everlasting. But then, what an undiminished time. Go into the solemn scenes of Job, and there, as if amid old solitudes and dim echoes of antiquity, converse with the inspired thoughts of God's existence. How the tide of song rolls in the Psalms with its mighty burden of truth, "Before the mountains were brought forth, or ever thou hadst formed the earth and the world, even from everlasting to everlasting, thou art God. For a thousand years are in thy sight but as yesterday when it is past and as a watch in the night." But scripture contains more than declarations of God's unnumbered years. It is also a history of his redemption, and we can now follow the upholdings of that vast purpose of love, the gospel. Now, one of the most impressive conclusions from such a course of thought, is the great extent of time employed in accomplishing the work of Christ. Though we can, from our point of observation, trace back, as in a line of light, the fully matured redemption to its promise, and germ in most primitive revelation; nay more, though we must believe, in so stupendous a providence as the salvation of a race, that "the Lamb of God was slain from the foundation of the world, yet its actual accomplishment on earth was seemingly long delayed. How time, to our view, was lavished on its history! Wearily the ages seem to wear away. The light dawned slowly on those centuries of darkness.

What long periods of apostacies and idolatries had first to pass! A mighty system of rites and ceremonies had to be elaborated, and to form a great school of preparation, and then to die out like the shell of a ripening germ. A national history of most varied events was first lived through. Prophets, in long succession, arose and pointed to a coming Saviour and died without seeing him of whom they wrote. But these years were as days, with the Lord. Time was not measured by him as we measure it, and therefore in its fullness Christ came. How natural for our impatient souls to exclaim, Oh, why came he not earlier! Why was not that promise fulfilled in a day. But the answer comes in lofty accents, "A thousand years with the Lord are as one day."

II. Turn we now to the world without us. This, too, is a revelation of God, and his works of creation tell the same tale of years. The geologist in his study of the deep earth, becomes awe struck at the proofs of the immense times apparent there. He sees, indeed, periods marked in growth, but then what almost profusion of duration! What ages God takes to form his beautiful gems! What time he gives for the perfection of his mineral riches! How many centuries have been lavished in the curious preparation of his gold and silver! What a record of ages is the treasure embedded in solid rock, and borne along in the course of old rivers! How have his great agents of fire and water, wrought in solitude and patience through vast periods, nor hasted their work as do short-lived men. And more solemn still, the record of times in the fossil histories of creation. There entombed in firm stone is a form that once sported in the sea. There are the monuments of animals that once moved in giant strength over this continent before the primitive men. Open that mass of coal, and there, finer than any artist's pencil can trace, is the outline of a plant that once waved in the breeze. What a lesson of years does the mine teach! Go deeper—deeper yet—everything shows that "a thousand years are as one day," with him who lavished such long times in preparing the things we burn. Listen to the tales of the waters. Where now the rich mould of the prairies waits for the husbandman, once flowed seas. This wondrous new world, as if made to receive the exhausted races of Europe, and afford a new probation to the nations, how long it was in making ready for the great emigrations of our centuries. Here mighty rivers, through remote ages, have been fertilizing the earth, and preparing a soil fit for the vast enterprize of later and greater empires.

It has been a long time since the natives of the South Seas planted themselves on those islands, but how lavish in his years, was God, ere the coral reefs rose silent and constant from the depths. None were there to tell the moments. But there was no haste. "A thousand years were as one day" with their Almighty architect. And now, ask the sailor whose weary eyes have looked long and anxiously for those islands, and whose feet have trod their grateful shores, if the work of ages is not wrought in Almighty beauty. What a creature of vast antiquity is that sublime ocean. How its very voice is eloquent of the immense past "far sounding" and mysterious! What changes it hath wrought for God! It has shaped the continents in beauty. It has curved and indented their shores. It has fed with its vapors mountain streams, and made fruitful lands remote from its tides. But all was done very slowly, as we think. It never hasted. It was God's faithful agent and it wrought through thousands of years. Go into the forests, and wander amid the aged pines: there are few sounds so full of dear to them! So now, if the stupendous problem of poverty is to be solved, it will demand sacrifices from which we shall assuredly shrink. It is vain to think of any other standard or test, than Christ. The cross of Christ in its fullest sense, is the grand rebuke of human selfishness. So is it the measure and example of human liberality. Yes, we must act in the spirit, aye up to it, of Christ. Look not then on others, but look where " He who was rich, became poor." Yes, think of Christ, the Holy Blessed One! See how he gave and then beholding the miseries of this world, and remembering what he has told us of his final judgment, ask if "we yet know what manner of spirit we are of." Again consider the grace of Christ as a motive to all duties. It is remarkable that in his exhortations to Christian virtues, Paul does not dwell so much on the usual moral grounds, but makes Christ the moving principle. The love of Christ, the sufferings of Christ, the judgment of Christ, above all, the spirit of Christ, these are the aspects which should affect the heart: Christ in all. On this the early teachers relied. There is great significance in this, and it indicates the methods we should follow with ourselves and others. Oh, if we could habitually contemplate Christ and apprehend him more clearly, be sure we should overcome our sins more thoroughly. Think you we could be so vindictive or worldly minded? So averse to duty in his service on earth, and most of all, so self-satisfied! Christ in view, would we not make more progress in divine life? So we have the grace of Christ as a means of awakening and converting men! There can be no doubt of the distinctive use of this truth by early Christians, for the end of reaching unawakened men. And certainly, we can see a fitness in this. True, men must be led by the law, but Christ, saving by grace, implies the law, while the wondrous majesty and supreme excellence of this Being, the love he manifested to men, the blessings he so freely proffers, ought above everything else, to affect the human heart. And it has wrought surpassing results. That any fail to yield to it is the crowning mystery of earth! Oh, how can any of you resist the grace of Christ? How withstand the appeal to your conscience, and the satisfaction of every highest want that comes from the view of such a Saviour? How remain so ungrateful to such a benefactor? Oh, think " of the grace of our Lord Jesus Christ!"

TIME WITH GOD

(Delivered June 20th, 1935.)

II Peter iii. 8. "One day is with the Lord as a thousand years, and a thousand years as one day."

PETER uttered this sublime word in view of the hasty conclusions formed by irreligious men who lived for present gratification, and feared only immediate consequences. They could not see the instant energy of God, and hence they presumptuously denied that energy. They measured time by the meanest limit, and confined judgment within meager periods. But this great scripture teaches how men should conceive of time as related to God, and presents the idea of retribution in its worthy scope. In abstract thought, indeed, an unfathomable mystery waits him who seeks to conceive of time, as in the mind of God. But this is only part of the whole mystery, how the finite at all is conceived of by God. When, from the essential point of pure deity, we strive to think resolutely of creation, we are lost. How the eternal, unchangeable Jehovah can come in contact with objects not existing before, his will create what was not at all in previous times, baffles utterly the reverent thinker. When we attempt to conciliate Providence, as we must of necessity recognize it, in ourselves and all around us, conducting events in endless succession, with the equally necessary idea of an infinite, changeless God, we are plunged into the unsearchable depths which scripture speaks of. "We cannot find out the Almighty unto perfection." We are ourselves such a mystery, finite beings with instinctive conceptions of the infinite. We cannot deny ourselves, or any parts of ourselves, and yet these two, so impossible to conciliate in mere thinking, are ourselves. But we must absolutely, if true to our real, existing natures, think of God as creating and exercising providence over his creation. If, then, we exist as his creatures, there are, relatively to him, a day and numbers of years. If he apprehend the existence of one man, he must apprehend the successive moments of that man's life. So, then, we must continue to apply these words in their plain sense to him, correcting our unworthy, and often dangerous, views of time, by scripture and the world without. Behold, then, our contracted notions of God's providence reproved in this proposition "A thousand years are with the Lord as one day." Ages are as clearly open to him as days. Centuries to come, reaching on beyond our power of imagination, nay, all duration, are embraced in his instantaneous glance. To us, the conception of many years is one of immensity. But God has no disproportionate estimates. The Being who lives forever cannot exaggerate the value of an age.

We separate events strangely. We do not hold strongly the intense relation of moral influences, we cannot attain such unities as his, but break up into independent histories, what is only one vast and inseparable whole. There are no such parts complete in themselves as we make. Thus men write their records and come to an end with each nation, and each period in national life, as if the ever continuing connection of events stopped there. So men read, and imagine they can understand, certain tracts of time without thought of a remoter past which has immensely determined this period so complacently studied. But, really, why is not America the continuation of the history of old Assyria?

times long past, as those dim melodies of the woods. If we may trust the science that investigates their age, there were many hundred years ere they stood up so huge and old. Whole generations of men passed away. They hurried through their existence, but there, through patient ages, those pines grew, and hardened, and became venerable. Even more impressive, are the conclusions from the heavens on this point. Whatever the true theories as to the formation of those bright worlds, there can be no doubt of the immense periods occupied in their changes. Their revolutions and disappearances from human eyes, till long years have passed; the light of newly discovered planets, requiring centuries to reach us; these illustrate the profusion of time with God. Thus scripture then, might just as fitly describe the processes of creation, as the course of judgment. Just as well might men cavil in this direction. So methinks I hear one say "Why was God so long in creation! Why now so lavish of the years! Why does he employ thousand of years to produce these natural changes, when he might accomplish them in a moment?" Even then might another object to a moment, as seen with more microscopic eye, and ask still, why so long, when God is as infinite in one direction of time as in another. "Oh why," might exclaim impatient man "why doth not God produce the mineral, the woods, in that, to us, inconceivable instant! Why these long and slow periods!" But no, the very men who refuse to believe God's full interest in human affairs, because results are not instantaneous, yet have to acknowledge the same fact in creation, graven on its rocks, and recorded on its trees, and solemnly discoursed by its ocean, that, "a thousand years are with the Lord as one day." Nor does this illustration fail in the world of mind and morals. Rather it is stronger because nearer the very matter of our scripture. Here, too, behold the same lavish expenditure of time. What years have been given to the establishment of great truths! Ages mark the progress of discovery. They who doubt the sure retribution of God, because of time, indicate the meaning of our text by their own histories of the arts. How many hundred years were consumed ere man was fully master of the great agents of physical progress. If the ancients had the compass and other means, yet how soon lost, or how imperfectly had, that centuries must pass ere men fully possessed them! How science faltered and came on slowly! But why was this? Why must such agents as printing and steam be so long in coming to the aid of human society? And now with the very elements whispering man's thoughts, and he ever standing on the verge of discoveries, why rises the veil over nature so slowly? Why are so many ages to be spent ere our race grasps what is meant for it? And still from the harmonies of science comes the same answer: "A thousand years are with the Lord as one day." Again why is God so profuse of years ere he gives the world his elect of mind? Millions of men of talent are there, but only here and there a man of genius. Unnumbered insects, with wings of petty fire, to sport on the edge of night, but only here and there a star in the firmament. A Homer, a Shakespeare, appears, and then a crowd of mere versifiers who play with words. One great thinker, and then a long and flat succession of inferior men who beat out his philosophy fine, and replace his life with mechanical imitations. The times are as long in the formation of real genius as in the products of earth and sea. Now, why is this so? Why should so many years pass before we see a real poet or thinker, men's crude attempts, meanwhile, only disappointing us? But the same lesson is taught still more impressively in the social progress of our race. For how slowly are great principles established! Through what discouraging alternations do they pass! Sometimes they seem gaining hold on the human mind, and then succeeds a disastrous time of rejection and defeat. Not one man or school of men, is ever so honored as to fix in clear light, a great principle. It is the work of long, painfully long, historical development. Thus, it was not one man nor one set of men who uttered distinctly the truth of religious liberty. Such pretensions may suit those who read history through the interpretations of sect, or who cherish a political saintdom, but cannot bide the observations of a large and true history. Providence has been long in maturing any grand elements of social truth, and even now, how humiliating is the reflection that a vast amount of human intelligence refuses to receive the teachings of history. Who might not weary at such perversity in men and wonder that such time is expended on the recognition of even theoretical truth! But still more painful is the slow progress of our race in actual elevation. Why is national freedom so long in being established on earth? And why must it be attended with such convulsive starts of revolution? And why do such anarchies seem perpetually to thrust the nations back? It seems as if the fruit never would ripen! Those embryos in Europe crushed under soldier and priest, ever failing, but ever struggling into form, that strange, slow thing in England, combining monarchy and oligarchy and democracy, with its parliamentary religion and popular heathenesse, penitent for other people's sins, and pharisaic for its own; —our own country, with its contradictions and oppositions. Why is so long time expended on this progress? Why so little real individuality, so much stagnancy or so wild and unhealthy a singularity? Why such dead conservatism clinging like the sloth to decayed trunks, or such reactions to the past, or such frenzied radicalism, earnest only to destroy? There is no true harmony yet, but antagonism reigns. How comes it that a mighty instinct ever urges our race onward, and Providence evidently bears us up to some great end and yet, the times are so immense in this work! Ages pass and still reactions follow each forward step, fearful condition of our progress. But so it is, and learn in face of God's great councils that, "A thousand years are with the Lord as one day."

This harmony in the revelation and works of God, once seen, we are prepared to appreciate his purely moral government. It is strange that any who receive without misgiving the rest of the order of Providence, should find difficulty with delay in its moral administration. For it is the same God here, and with him "a thousand years are as one day". His long course of retribution is in perfect agreement with this idea. The Bible says he waited a hundred years ere he poured on the world the wrathful deluge. Ages, too, passed before the prophetic doom fell on those guilty empires of antiquity. They were huge fabrics of blood, and ambition, and idolatry. They sinned for whole generations. It was very long before their ruin came. Yet now we can trace that ruin from its doom. The time only makes the vindication more apparent. Slow but sure was the progress of retribution. Well may God employ his thousand years; it is as a day. There is the same connection of causes. The principles indicated on this stupendous scale, are just the same as if brought out in a moment of time. There is nothing but this circumstance of time to distinguish the fall of guilty empires from the instant execution of a criminal. It required many years to build huge Babylon, but the last brick has not yet mouldered away, and it were just as true to deny the natural law which assures its decay, because working through so many centuries, as the moral law which accomplishes its doom, because executed through so long a period. The proof of folly blasted, and impiety doomed, is just as perfect as though each stone had in an hour been smitten back to dust. So may we use modern history. Find if you can, one great law of right that has not been vindicated, or is not in progress of retribution. Ah the law bides its time! From the first moment of its insult, the seeds of judgment were planted, and God watched them and carried on their culture for the terrible harvest. Oh it is as unphilosophical as immoral to think of God as constrained to indicate his government within the scope of our moments. Would we appreciate Providence, we must look at God in the sublime light of "the ancient of days." Surely no thoughtful man can help seeing that we are amid processes and results of national retribution. Sometimes we can trace through many years the sure conduct of people, to suffering. If wrong principles are implanted in a nation they will come out. There is time enough for it. Occasionally a flash from behind the clouds, a heaving of the earth, tells us Providence, like a mighty elaborator is at work in sleepless ages. Keep fast hold of eternal principles of right and be sure they will at last show themselves vindicated. For the years will not loose their solemn charge. Not one shall be swallowed up in the abyss of ages. Inf. 1. The view we have taken may better enable us to understand that scripture which under the simple figure of "the little leaven leavening the whole lump," teaches the progress of Christianity. Some may affect to ask why was not this religion established full orbed at the first. They who ask this question are shut up to what they learn from nature, and viewed thus, the history of the gospel is in harmony with all nature. Like that it came from one with whom "a thousand years is as one day." If it had completed the restoration of man, according to this notion, it had been unlike all else of God's works. Now read its progress. How long it was before it gained firm hold of the nations. What centuries of alternate successes and reverses before it triumphed over paganism. How slowly it has won its way into the tangled heart of human society. How impossible to hasten its progress by human supplements. The human cannot increase the divine. Men think to promote it by making it local and embedding it in the State, and incorporating sinners into it, and baptizing those whom God has not baptized. But as a keen thinker once said of one who attempted to turn a great national movement to his own selfish purpose. It did not mean that, Christianity does not mean churchdoms, it means men truly regenerate by the Holy Spirit. So there is no hurrying the gospel of Christ. It is indeed natural for us to grow weary, and wonder why God does not at once convert the world to himself. But we forget that we are speaking of him "with whom a thousand years are as one day." Great conditions, physical and social, which we do not expect to see fulfilled in an age, and which we learn are little understood by us, need to be answered. Immense changes must come, that men cannot hasten, though they struggle in agony. But let this, our text, teach us that the great formations below and above are moving on, and the new creation of God is advancing through the ages. Strange that good men are so impatient to see the world come to its end. Christianity does not hasten its work, and so they interpret scripture to fortell a speedy doom. Even impulsive Peter found sublime repose in the truth we have been studying. So may we. Oh, time is a mighty thing in the providence of God. With it he matures and seals his great creation. Nothing is strong or enduring unblessed of time. The ages are alone the sufficient discipline of humanity, and earth shall not be unripely gathered. It is indeed very sad to see men refuse this faith; to look on characters growing in sin, unchanged, wasting probation. A terrible thing that men like you will reject such a salvation. But if you will not accept the gospel, and these passing Sabbaths shall go unblessed, "why a thousand years with the Lord are as one day." Other men, nobler than you, shall yet give themselves to Christ, when all of us have been gone long years. Oh, up from moments of formality, and money seeking, and forgotten vows, and unrealities, we look into the future and see the Spirit of God poured out from on high. It comes in light and life, breathing fresh vigor and beauty. It creates souls in holiness, and they come like stars out of the darkness mid the glad welcomings of the Sons of God.

Inf. II. Irreligious men may learn from this scripture not to be secure in their sins. You live in the government of the "ancient of days." Of what moment is it when he visits your sin! Have you done wrong to your neighbor, defrauded or slandered him? What if years have rolled by, and prosperity has poured its stores around you, and you are entrenched as with a rampart! Perhaps before you die that sin may find you out. There is great terror in the thought of one who waits so long! Are you now practising any iniquity? Do you walk among men and wear a calm face and even keep a still heart? What of that? What if conscience sleeps for a long time? What is time with the God against whom you sin? Time enough yet for judgment. Keep then that firm heart, walk on just as if all were well. Look the pure and the good in the face with an untroubled eye. If a pang of horror at times steals up from secret depths within you and casts a shadow of retribution over your spirit, scourge it back; all is quiet yet. Long years have passed over your ungodly life. Longer yet, may. Perhaps *He* will forget you! Fool, it is the more frightful that he waits so long. Oh, how can any man live reckless of Jesus Christ, toiling for money, chasing pleasure, and think of an immense future with any calmness? But no, you do not think. You dare not think of those ages, and of plunging into them with your lives all unrepented. You shrink from that immensity. Oh, what a thought is these vast years! How will earth appear? What time in which to correct reasoning! All impatience checked! And we shall never chide the coming ages. In happiness or anguish, we shall master this truth, that a "thousand years are as one day." What folly for men to hate, to trifle, to live for earth, when they may be just on the verge of these years beyond the grave!

www.ingramcontent.com/pod-product-compliance
Lightning Source LLC
Chambersburg PA
CBHW021732220426
43662CB00008B/821